# You too can change the world

## Daphne Spraggett with Jill Johnstone

WEC International
Bulstrode, Gerrards Cross
Bucks, SL9 8SZ, U.K.

# CONTENTS

# INTRODUCTION

One grey November day in 1991 I stood on a hill overlooking a sprawling city in the Near East. As I gazed down my heart was filled with great sadness. In that city of 100,000 people there were only two Christians. Some people living there have heard the name of Jesus but only a few of them understand that he is God's Son who came to earth to show men and women the true way to find God.

I stood on the hillside and prayed for the people in that city. Suddenly I remembered that Jesus had looked over another city – Jerusalem. He loved the people there. He wanted to protect them like a mother hen who shelters her chicks from danger. But they would not come to him. Would the people in the city below me ever come to Jesus?

I prayed for the people of that city then, and I still pray for them. I believe my prayers are helping to change the lives of men and women there. I am sure that one day there will be many more than two people in that city who know and love Jesus.

## About this book

There are about 230 COUNTRIES in our world. The people who live in them belong to thousands of smaller groups who speak different languages and have different customs. Sometimes they have come from other places and have settled in the country they now call their homeland. These are called PEOPLE GROUPS. In the country of India alone, there are at least 4,635 people groups and 1,652 different languages are spoken.

In this book you will read about 26 countries and 26 people groups. This means that there is a chapter for you to read every week of the year. Each chapter has stories, information and pictures to help you understand a little of what life is like in these countries and among the various people groups.

You might want to read these chapters on your own or with your families and friends, and together find out all you can about the country or people group for that week. Watch the news and programmes about other countries on TV. Look in newspapers and books for extra information. The more we know and understand, and the more we let what we know burn in our hearts, the better we can pray!

At the end of each section there are seven prayer points, one for every day of the week. (Of course, you can pray them all on one day.) As you read you will probably want to make up your own prayers as well.

Keep your eyes and ears open for the answers to your prayers. Sometimes you will think nothing is happening. Don't stop praying. Sometimes you have to wait a long time to see answers, but you will discover that your prayers are helping to change countries, people groups, situations and individuals. That is exciting! And remember to thank God for answering your prayers.

## Why should we pray?

Why does God want us to pray? We often hear people say that God could work without our prayers because he is the King of kings and Lord of lords. But God does want us to pray because he wants us to share in his work in the world. How do we know that? When we read the Bible we find God tells us to pray (e.g. Luke 10:2) and we see that he answers prayer (e.g. Acts 16:25-34).

In this book you will find examples of countries that have been changed, or are being changed, because people prayed and went on praying, sometimes for years and years. Russia is one of those countries and Vietnam is another.

## To help you pray

• Prayer is simply talking with God and he longs for us to talk to him. As we pray and learn to listen to him, we get to know and love him more and more. And when we pray, we are working with God and helping him to change the world.

• We can pray anywhere and at any time. We don't even need to put our hands together and close our eyes, or even to use special words. I often pray as I go for a walk or when I am working. When I wake up in the middle of the night, I pray quietly in my bed.

•We can talk to God about all the things that trouble us. As we talk with him, he helps us to know what to do because he knows everything.

•Sometimes we pray and pray, but don't SEE anything happening for a long while. Why is that? If you plant a bulb it takes a long while before you see anything, but underground the shoot is beginning to grow, and one day you'll see it. Prayer is like that.

•We have to remember, too, that Satan wants people and countries to belong to him rather than to God. He even tempted Jesus to do things his way, not God's way (Matthew 4:1-11). So don't give up – but keep on praying!

• God wants us to be his friends, but sometimes we do things that do not please him. Perhaps we have said or done things which have hurt other people. We may have been selfish and forgotten to help others. We have to put these things right and say we are sorry for the things we have done wrong. Then God hears and answers (Psalm 66:18).

•God wants us to trust him to answer our prayers (Matthew 21:22). That is very important.

So let us pray – and help change the world.

## TO HELP YOU

• Christianity and Judaism, two of the world's great religions, are explained on pages 114 and 115.

• You will find the meanings of difficult words in this book in the Word List on pages 116-117.

• You will find a map of the world on pages 124-125.

• On page 118 you will find some ideas to help you, your family and Sunday School, to get involved in missionary work now.

• Sometimes you will want to learn more about the countries and people groups you are praying for. On page 122 I have listed some Christian organizations who may be able to help you.

### This is what to do:
1. Decide what you want to find out about. If you want to ask about a people group, you must first find out what country they are in. Next find out from the list which agencies may be able to help you. You will find their addresses on page 123.

2. When you write, ask about only one or two people groups or countries at a time. Say what you want to know, and why you want to find out more. Ask what materials they have and tell them how you will use it (at home, Sunday School or club).

3. It is important that you write at least a month before you need materials or information. (They could have lots of letters at the same time, or they may send your letter to someone else.)

4. *Remember that it costs money to help you, so be ready to pay for what is sent to you.*

# AFGHANISTAN

## A LAND AT WAR WITH ITSELF

### All alone!

Ramazan edged out of the ruins of his home in Kabul, the capital of war-torn Afghanistan. A government truck, loaded with wheat, sped by. Quick as a flash, Ramazan rushed out to gather a few grains that had trickled out from the load. It was only a handful – but better than having nothing to eat at all. He was alone. His parents and brother had all been killed when a mortar shell destroyed their home.

Afghanistan, in the heart of Central Asia, is a harsh place. High mountains and desert, hot, dry summers and very cold winters make life very hard. Over many centuries it has been a place of fierce battles. The Persians, ancient Greeks, Mongols and Turks, and later the British and the Soviets, have all invaded Afghanistan. To make matters worse, there has always been fighting between the powerful Pushtun people, and the Tajik, Hazara, Uzbek and other tribes living in the country. After a pro-Communist coup in 1978, the Soviet Union invaded Afghanistan, and millions of Afghans fled to the neighbouring countries of Iran and Pakistan. Ten years later the Soviets withdrew their forces.

### War and suffering

'But why is there still fighting?' Saud, Ramazan's friend, asked his father. 'Who is the enemy now?'

'When the Communists came,' his father replied, 'we fought a *jihad*, a Muslim holy war against them. Many of us became *mujahidin* guerrillas to get rid of them. They have gone now, but the fighting goes on because each group of *mujahidin* wants to be the most powerful and lead our country. As a result we all suffer. Although we are all Muslims, we do not trust one another.

'My father told me about some Christians who came to help our people. They operated on blind people's eyes so that they could see again. Our government demolished their church. That is how we rewarded them for their help. Some people say that ever since then God has been judging Afghanistan. I sometimes wonder why Christians from other countries still live here and help us through their aid programmes.'

Many people around the world are praying for Afghanistan. Their prayers are being answered, and some Afghans are becoming Christians.

## DO YOU KNOW?

The night after he ordered the only Christian church in Afghanistan to be destroyed, the king was dethroned.

8

## Fearless

Mehmet* is a Christian truck driver. He was given some Dari New Testaments. (Dari is one of the main languages spoken in Afghanistan). Wherever he stopped, Mehmet talked to people about Jesus. He knew he could be killed for doing this, but he also knew that following Jesus was the most important thing in his life. 'Read this book,' he told interested people, giving them a New Testament. On his return journey he would look out for those same people. Some had become Christians.

*Not his real name.*

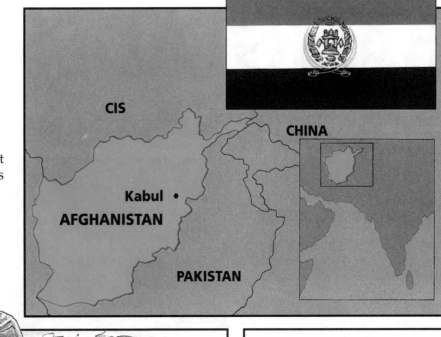

# Counting the cost

Zia was born a Muslim. He was blind and, when he was 14 years old he went to the Institute for the Blind in Kabul. He was very clever and already knew the whole of the Koran by heart in Arabic. He learned English by listening to English programmes on his radio. His favourite programme was 'Voice of the Gospel'.

Zia became a Christian, but when he told his friends they were shocked. 'You know that Islamic law says that anyone who leaves Islam must be put to death,' they said. Zia answered, 'I have counted the cost and am willing to die for the Messiah, since Jesus has already died on the cross for me.'

When the Communists came to power, Zia refused to join them. He was put in prison. How glad he was that he had his overcoat with him, because there were no blankets and the prisoners had to sleep on the freezing mud floor. Another prisoner was shivering with cold, so Zia gave him his coat. He was tortured but would not give in to the Communists' demands. Eventually he was freed and escaped to Pakistan, where he worked hard, translating the Old Testament into Dari and helping other Afghan refugees.

Fanatical Afghan Muslims kidnapped Zia, tortured him and beat him for hours because he was a Christian. Only his captors know what happened to him. Many people believe that Zia has died and is now wonderfully happy in heaven.

## You Can Pray for Afghanistan

**Dear Lord Jesus**

1 Please bring peace to Afghanistan.

2 Make the *mujahidin* realize that they are destroying both their country and their people.

3 Be with the Christian aid workers as they help people who are suffering and hurting as a result of the civil war. May their love show the blind, injured, sick and needy how much you care for them.

4 May those who have become Christians know that you are always with them, even when they are punished for following you.

5 When people receive a New Testament in Pushto or Dari, may your Holy Spirit teach them to understand your Word.

6 Help and protect those who are translating the Scriptures into other Afghan languages.

7 As people listen to Christian radio programmes, help them to understand what they hear and to find you as Saviour, just as Zia did.

# BANGLADESH

## ONE OF THE POOREST COUNTRIES ON EARTH

### Homeless

Chandra sat by his father on the heap of mud where their home had once stood. The chicken he clutched in his arms squawked and struggled to escape. Aziz, his father, gripped a small basket of rice. This was all they had managed to save when floodwaters from the huge Brahmaputra River, and lashing rain and whirling winds from the south, had destroyed their home.

Aziz sighed. 'When the floods come, they bring fresh soil and make the land fertile so we can grow good crops. When the winds come and the rains are heavy, they destroy everything – our homes, our cattle – and many people die. I don't know what has happened to your mother and little sister. Perhaps they are safe; perhaps they are dead.'

'What shall we do now?' Chandra asked.

'We'll start again,' his father replied. 'What has happened is the will of *Allah*. We'll go to Dhaka. Perhaps you will be able to find work in the market. You may even be able to go to school. I don't know what I shall do, because I cannot read or write.'

BANGLADESH
• Dhaka

INDIA

• Chittagong

BAY OF BENGAL

# God has his ways to help!

About twenty years ago a Christian who was visiting Bangladesh asked God how he could help the poor people there. Then he realized that they could use local materials to make handicrafts to sell in other countries! Now Tearcraft (a part of Tear Fund) helps many people there to earn a living. Perhaps you have been to a special Tearcraft evening in your church and have bought some of the lovely goods on sale. You may even have bought a jute *sika* or hanging plant-holder for your mother.

In Bangladeshi homes *sikas* are used to hold vegetables, eggs or anything else that needs to be kept off the floor and out of the way. It is quite easy to make a *sika*, but growing the jute and getting it ready for use is really hard work.

Shaheen and his family grow jute in one of their fields. 'Jute is grown in water, like rice,' Shaheen explains, 'but it grows much taller than rice. A good crop will grow three or four metres high. Each thick stalk holds the jute fibres.

'When it is time for harvest, the men and boys cut down the heavy stalks and take them by boat or ox-cart to their homes. The women arrange the jute stalks in huge, round stacks to dry. The smell is awful! When the jute is dry, everyone in the family has to help beat the stalks, until all the fibres come loose. Ee! We all get so hot and tired and dirty. Even then it's not ready for use.

'Christian groups often buy the jute and sell it to the village women and girls to make things such as *sikas*, bags and mats, to sell in other countries. My wife and daughters like making these things. Sometimes the people who come to buy these things tell them about God's love. Sometimes I wonder if what they tell us is true. Our lives have been so much better since they started to help us in this way.'

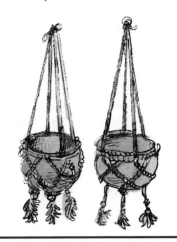

## Floods and mighty winds

Every year in Bangladesh it rains from May to October. Every year, when the snows on the Himalayan mountains melt, the water comes rushing down the mighty Ganges, Brahmaputra and Meghna Rivers to the sea. Every year the rivers burst their banks and flood the land, bringing fresh soil to the fertile land. Every year homes and fields are washed away by the swirling flood-waters, and animals and people die. When a cyclone batters the country, the chaos and destruction are terrible.

It is no wonder that Bangladesh is one of the poorest countries in the world. There are so many rivers, so little land and so many people that it is also one of the most crowded countries on earth. Everyone, from the smallest child to the oldest grandfather, has to work hard just to live.

Most Bangladeshis are Muslims, but some are Hindus. For many years Christians have run hospitals and schools. They have done all they can to help when disasters come, but there are still very few Bangladeshi Christians. That does not stop Christians from helping because they know that the people of Bangladesh are important to Jesus.

## You Can Pray for Bangladesh

### Dear Lord Jesus

1 Use Christian workers to show the people of Bangladesh that you do care for them and want to help them.

2 Help the leaders of this country, which suffers so much during the monsoons, to be honest, wise and fair in everything.

3 Thank you for the work of TEAR Fund. Please use the handicraft projects to help people understand your love for them.

4 Bring revival to the small church in Bangladesh. May all who say they are Christians become truly yours.

5 Train young men and women who are studying in Bible Schools to be good witnesses for you and able to teach others about you.

6 Call out Christians who can work with the many homeless children and young people in Bangladesh.

7 May many Bangladeshis who live in other countries meet Christians who can lead them to know you.

# BULGARIA

## HUNGRY FOR GOD

### Following Jesus

'Why do you keep going to that Protestant church?' Theodor's father demanded. 'Haven't you seen what's written about them in the newspapers, or heard on the radio or T.V. what they're like? They're dangerous. We don't want you kidnapped or harmed. If you want to go to church, go to the Orthodox church. After all, that's the State Church.'

Theodor is a new Christian. A few months earlier a friend had taken him to an evangelistic campaign where Luis Palau was speaking. There, for the first time in his life, he heard that Jesus loves him and died for him on the Cross at Calvary.

'What should I do?' Theodor wondered. 'It's not easy to follow Jesus when so many bad things are said about the Protestants. The leaders of the Orthodox churches wouldn't even allow a Protestant mission ship to come here. Some of them even threatened to board the ship and throw all the evangelical literature into the sea.'

### Are we free?

From 1949 until 1989 Bulgaria was a communist country and the government tried to stop people from going to church. They followed Russia's laws so closely that it became known as 'Little Russia'.

When communism fell, everyone hoped there would be freedom for all the churches in the country, and for a little while this was so. Many people came to trust in Jesus. Soon, however, the new socialist government announced that the Orthodox faith was the religion of Bulgaria. All other denominations were *sects* and were not wanted! Today, two-thirds of the people living in Bulgaria belong to the Orthodox Church.

12

## Bibles for all!

But God wants Bulgarians to know him for themselves. In 1994 the Minister of Culture and Education gave permission for Bibles to be given to every school child. How eagerly the children accepted this gift. Eleven-year-old Slavi, who lived in an orphanage, was so happy when he was given a Bible that he started to read it at once. Even when he was given a bar of chocolate he did not look up until he had finished the story he was reading.

## Jesus visited me

Almost a million and a quarter of the people living in Bulgaria are Muslims. Some, the Pomaks, are true Bulgarians. Others have

### DO YOU KNOW?

A special Turkish New Testament in Cyrillic (Russian-style) script has been produced for the Bulgarian Turks. Although they speak Turkish, they cannot read the romanized script (like ours) of modern Turkish.

come from Turkey. Another group, the Millet, are gypsies. Many Bulgarian Turks and gypsies are coming to know Jesus.

Ahmed's family are Bulgarian Turks. 'I always wanted to serve *Allah*,' he said, 'so I learned to read Arabic and studied the Koran. In some places the Koran speaks very highly of Jesus.

'When I was ten or eleven years old I had a dream I have never forgotten. God and Jesus visited our house and I had to look after them. Jesus wanted to give me a jar of water, but I was afraid he would go away if I took it. He promised he would never leave me, so I took the jar.

'About nine years later I met a man who was arguing with other men that Jesus was greater than Mohammed. He gave me a very old, tatty, Turkish Bible. Although I read it, I could not understand it, and became ill. I wrote to the man: "You have planted a little tree in my heart. Why do you not come to water it?" When he came to visit me he could not help me, because he was not really a Christian.

'I thought that perhaps God would help me to understand the

Bible, so I prayed to him. When I opened the Bible, I read the story in John 4 where Jesus promises to give living water. Immediately I remembered my dream of long ago. From then onwards I only wanted to follow Jesus.

'I wanted my family to follow Jesus so much, but they wouldn't. Some years later my son had an accident, and the doctors said he would lose an eye. I prayed in Jesus' Name, and God healed him. When my family saw that Jesus healed my son they wanted to follow Jesus, as well.

'Yes, Jesus is helping people to get to know God here in Bulgaria.'

### You Can Pray for Bulgaria

#### Dear Lord Jesus

1 May your Holy Spirit help every true believer to be bold in witnessing for you, even when wrong things are said about them.

2 Help Bulgarian Turks who have become Christians to forgive the communists who took away their rights and forced them to have Bulgarian names.

3 Make it possible for every church leader and pastor to have good Bible training so that they will be able to teach Christians to follow you in the right way.

4 Give many people dreams and visions, so that they will know you are the true God.

5 May your Holy Spirit help children to enjoy reading the Bibles that have been given them. May they learn to love your Word and to obey it.

6 Please use organizations like Scripture Union and Child Evangelism Fellowship to teach the children how to follow you.

7 Help all the churches and Christian groups from other countries to work together in love so that many more Bulgarians will be drawn to you.

# CHINA

## HOME TO A FIFTH OF THE WORLD'S PEOPLE!

### No religions!

'The time has come when we must leave China. The communists are trying to get rid of all foreign influences in this country. Although we would like to stay to help the church, the Christians will suffer even more persecution if we do!'

It was the end of 1950. The communists had taken power in China and millions of people had been executed. Many of those who were killed were land-owners and people with businesses, Christians and those who had studied at Christian schools and colleges.

With tears in their eyes and great sadness in their hearts, the missionaries left China. During the previous 140 years, thousands of missionaries had faced many hardships to bring the Good News of the gospel to China. Some had been killed, others beaten, stoned, robbed or put in prison.

Had all their work been useless? Would the church die? What would happen to the Christians they had left behind? Would they remember all they had been taught of the Christian faith? There were many godly pastors, but would they be allowed to teach and evangelize? The communists aimed to get rid of all religions. Would they succeed?

### Standing firm

Although the door into China had slammed shut and many terrible things were happening to the people of China, God knew what he would do! There was not much news about the church or the Christians, but all round the world people prayed and prayed for China, and kept on praying. God was at work!

As they faced persecution, many of the Chinese Christians stood firm for Jesus. During the Cultural Revolution (1966-1990) some of their leaders were killed. Others were put in prison or sent to labour camps. They were brain-washed and tortured in an attempt to make them say they did not belong to Jesus. However harshly they were treated, they would not deny their Saviour! Quietly in their homes they talked about the love of Jesus, and of the help and strength he gave them. Instead of being stamped out, the church in China continued to grow.

At last the door into China opened a little way. Soon Chinese people living in other parts of the world were allowed to visit their relatives in China. Yes, there were many Christians among them. They secretly took Bibles with them and prayed with their families. They brought back the news that the Chinese church was growing and growing. Christians met in homes wherever they could, to pray to God, to worship him and learn more about him.

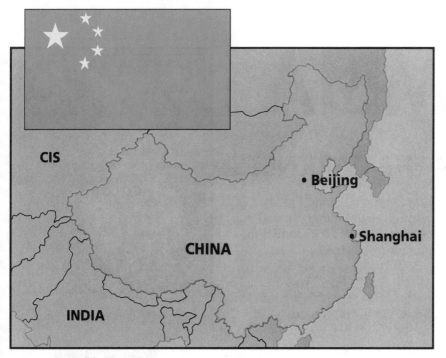

## DO YOU KNOW?

Only Russia and Canada cover a bigger land area than China, but China has the largest population of any country in the world. There are at least 56 people groups living in China.

## You Can Pray for China

**Dear Lord Jesus**

1 Thank you for all the missionaries who have worked in China, and for answering the prayers of those who have prayed for that land.

2 Thank you for the many Christians who kept on following you even when they were treated badly because they belonged to you.

3 May Chinese children hear about you from their Christian friends and families. Please make it possible for them to have Sunday Schools.

4 Help Christian families to be good examples to all who live near them.

5 May your Holy Spirit work in the hearts of young people and bring them to know you as their Saviour. Make them eager to learn all they can about you and your love for them.

6 Make it possible for Bible Schools to be set up, so that more Christians can be trained as pastors and evangelists.

7 May there be leaders in China who will rule this huge country wisely and with justice.

## A hidden Book

Yang is seven years old. Like most children in China, he has no brothers or sisters because there is a law which says that each family may have only one child. Yang's parents are both Christians, and, when other Christians come to their home, Yang likes to sit in a corner and listen as they read the Bible and pray. After their visitors have left Yang usually begs his father to tell him another story from the Bible.

'Tell me again how God created the world. At school the teachers tell us that we grew from monkeys.' Yang's father takes his Bible from its hiding place and starts to read. 'I wish some of my friends could come and listen to these stories,' Yang pleads.

'You know there is a law which forbids us to teach the gospel to children,' his father explains. 'All the same, if one or two of your friends came here sometimes, I could tell them some Bible stories. Go and fetch one of them now, but be quiet about it!'

## Church alive!

The communists thought they could stamp out religion in China. Although they have treated Christians very harshly, the church has not disappeared, as they expected. Instead, it has grown and grown. No-one knows exactly how many Christians there are now in China, but it is thought that there are millions more than when the missionaries had to leave in 1950.

Yes, God is answering all those prayers for China, and the Chinese Christians know that, however hard their life may be, nothing will ever be able to separate them from God's love.

# COLOMBIA

## LIGHT SHINES IN THE DARKNESS

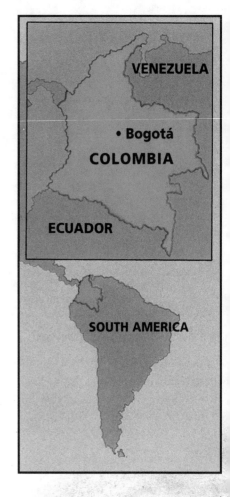

'Please tell the children good things about Colombia as well as the bad,' my friend pleaded. 'So many people think of Colombia only as a land of begging, stealing, smuggling, killing, dying and drugs. It's true that violence is a part of life in Colombia, but it's a beautiful land and most Colombians are warm and loving people. Evangelical Christians have been persecuted for their faith, but now more people than ever are putting their trust in Jesus.'

Colombia, in the north-west corner of South America, is the fourth largest country in that continent. Coffee and oil production and trade with other countries have brought wealth to Colombia. Gold, platinum and emeralds are mined, but these precious materials have often been the cause of bitter violence.

A hundred years ago Colombia was one of the poorest countries in South America. That is changing now. Some people have become very rich, but many are still very poor.

### God is Love

Six-year-old Paolo and her little brother Freddy are two poor children living in Bogota, the capital city. Their mother is a drug-addict. Their father used to sort through rubbish for things he could sell, such as paper and bottles, so that he could buy food for his family. He was often drunk, but he loved his children.

They lived in a small, dark room in a part of the city which is often called 'the doorway to hell'. When their parents went out at night, they locked the children in

that room. Paolo and Freddy often felt cold, hungry and alone. During the day they roamed the danger-filled streets.

A Christian day-care school called 'God is Love' was opened in this slum area. 'It's a good place,' Paolo and Freddy's parents said. 'We want you to go there, then you won't need to wander the city streets on your own. The people are kind and will give you good, hot food to eat.'

Paolo and Freddy enjoyed going to school. The teachers taught them to read and told them about God's love. That message of love spoke to their parents, too.

One day another man killed their father. Their mother seized the children and ran to the 'God is Love' school. There they were looked after, but one day their mother said, 'I cannot stop taking drugs so I must go away. Please look after Paolo and Freddy for me. Help them to know God's love.'

Christians are opening other schools and homes in the poorest, most godless parts of the city so that children like Paolo and Freddy may be given hope for a better life.

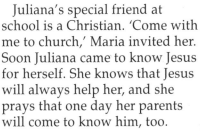

## A poor rich child

Juliana is also a Colombian child, but she has everything she wants or needs. She goes to a private school and spends most weekends with her aunts and grandparents in the country. Every summer she visits her cousins in the United States.

Her father is a brilliant and wealthy lawyer. He is also an alcoholic. When her parents were divorced, Juliana was very sad. 'Who will help me?' she wondered. Her parents are Catholics but, like many Colombians, they hardly ever go to church.

Juliana's special friend at school is a Christian. 'Come with me to church,' Maria invited her. Soon Juliana came to know Jesus for herself. She knows that Jesus will always help her, and she prays that one day her parents will come to know him, too.

## Light in prison

Until recently Medellín was one of the most violent cities in Colombia. It has a maximum security prison called Bellavista, or 'Beautiful View', which is full of thieves, murderers and drug pushers.

Only one man was brave enough to visit the prisoners. Oscar Osorio had once been in prison himself, then he became a Christian. There, in that overcrowded, dangerous place, Oscar declares that Jesus can change lives and set men and women free from the power of sin and evil. Many people have asked God to do that for them. Now they are studying God's Word in their own Bible School in prison.

God is changing lives in Colombia. That's why my friend asked me to tell you about the good things in Colombia as well as the bad! Men and women, boys and girls, whether they are poor or rich, good or bad, are finding out that God loves them and makes their lives new when they trust in him.

## DO YOU KNOW?

As well as natural resources like oil and gold, Colombia is rich in plant and animal life. It has 1,721 species of birds, the highest recorded number in any country in the world.

## You Can Pray for Colombia

### Dear Lord Jesus

1 May many people who are angry, hurt and afraid discover that you can comfort and help them.

2 Give Christian leaders in the government wisdom to help their country and courage to speak out for what is right.

3 May your Holy Spirit give Christians who truly know you the power to live honest and holy lives.

4 Defeat the power of Satan, so that violence, drugs and evil living will no longer be such a strong influence in Colombian life.

5 As you change people's lives by your almighty power, give their friends courage to trust in you so that their lives will be changed, too.

6 May every child who lives on the streets or in the slums meet Christians who will help them to know and understand your love.

7 May all the churches work together to make your love known.

# CUBA

## LAND OF BEAUTY, LAND OF NEED

### Sugar and slaves

Did you know that Christopher Columbus discovered the beautiful Caribbean island of Cuba in 1492, the year in which he discovered America? A few years later the Spanish *conquistadors* (conquerors) claimed it for Spain. The Spaniards who settled on this fertile, tropical island quickly established sugar plantations.

They needed people to work on the plantations, so they shipped thousands of black slaves across the Atlantic Ocean from West Africa. Slavery was abolished just over a hundred years ago, and many of the people who live in Cuba now are descendants of those slaves. Even when Cuba became an independent country, many former slaves continued to live and work on the sugar plantations.

Sugar made many people very wealthy, and by 1959 Cuba was the richest country in Latin America. Thousands of tourists came from North America, attracted by the luxury of cities such as Havana. There they spent their time gambling and drinking.

But not everyone was rich. There were thousands of very poor people who wanted homes and enough food and clothing for their families. They certainly could not afford to send their children to school.

### Revolution and education

On January 1st 1959 Fidel Castro and his *guerrillas* overthrew the government. They wanted to make Cuba a better country. They began by making sure that every child went to school, and adults were taught to read, too.

Roberto was eight years old when the revolution took place. 'We went to school in a hut,' he said. 'I was excited. I was told I would get a good job if I learned to read. My family were very poor. We didn't have shoes, and had only old, ragged clothes to wear. We didn't have enough food and were often very hungry. A good job would mean we'd have more to eat and better clothes to wear.'

He smiled sadly. 'The revolution didn't really help us very much. The United States of America stopped trading with us because we were Communists. The Russians helped us, but they're not helping us any more. I am still very poor. My children are hungry and don't have good clothes.'

'Some people have become rich because they have friends in the United States who send them dollars, but we have no one. Some of our friends work in Havana at one of the special hotels for rich tourists, but there are not many jobs. Cuba is a very beautiful island. It is also a land of great need.'

### Witchcraft

Cuba is a Communist country, but almost half the people say they are Christians. However, very few people go to church. Almost a quarter of the people practise *Sanetarie,* a form of witchcraft, in which they worship evil spirits and make animal sacrifices. They are afraid of the spirits, which often make them do strange and frightening things. Wonderfully, some are finding that Jesus can set them free from the tight grip of Satan.

### Following Jesus

After the revolution in 1959, police informers seemed to be everywhere. Christians were often persecuted and put in prison because they continued to follow Jesus.

'We remembered that Jesus loves us and has done so much for us,' Gregorio said. 'We loved

• Havana
ATLANTIC OCEAN
CUBA
CARIBBEAN SEA

## You Can Pray for Cuba

### Dear Lord Jesus

1 Please give Christians the freedom to meet together.

2 May there soon be enough Bibles for every Christian to have one.

3 Please provide work, food and clothes for those who are poor.

4 Please use Christian radio programmes to bring many people to know you.

5 Use organizations in other countries to send Christian books to the pastors and preachers.

6 Help Christians not to be afraid of telling others about you.

7 Show people who practise *Sanetarie* that it is wrong. May your Holy Spirit set them free from the power of the devil.

him, too, and knew that we must obey him and not be afraid. We were so glad that we could listen to Christian radio broadcasts, even when we could not meet together in church.

'Now there is more freedom and many young people and children are excited to discover that Jesus loves them. They are on fire for Jesus! Often the children meet together in their homes to worship God and to learn from his Word. They even organize their own special meetings without grown-ups to help them.'

I expect you have a Bible, but in Cuba only a few Christians have even a New Testament. How they long to have one so that they can read God's Word! Christians in other Latin American countries and in North America and Europe have organized special campaigns to raise money so that Bibles can be sent to Cuba. Can you imagine the excitement when a Cuban Christian receives a Bible for himself?

# EGYPT

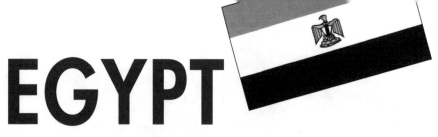

## POVERTY AND WEALTH IN AN ANCIENT LAND

### A rubbish-dump village

'Wonder what we'll find today?' Dirty and ragged, Fuad and Ramzi sat on top of the big pile of rotting, stinking rubbish in their father's donkey-cart. As the old donkey plodded wearily along, cars, trucks and buses, blaring their horns, passed them on the busy Cairo street.

Early that morning, just as they did every morning, Fuad and Ramzi had gone with their father to collect rubbish from the city streets. Their village is on the outskirts of Cairo, not many miles from the ancient pyramids. It is one huge rubbish tip. They were quite used to the filth and stench, for they had lived in the rubbish-dump village all their lives.

Carefully, Fuad and Ramzi sorted the rubbish. Anything that could be eaten, they took to their mother in their little hut made from cardboard and flattened tins. Anything they could sell, they put in one heap, and anything they could use in another. Anything that was no use at all was left for the dogs and cats to nose through for food.

### Millionaires

In Cairo, the capital of Egypt, there are more than a million people who, like Fuad and Ramzi and their parents, scratch a living from the rubbish of the fourteen million other people who live there. About half the people in Cairo are very poor and live in slums. Many rich people live there too, and at least 200,000 of them are millionaires.

### Survival

On the day of Pentecost there were Egyptians in Jerusalem who heard Jesus' disciples tell of God's love for all people, and what his Son, Jesus, had done for them. When they went back to Egypt they took the Christian faith with them. The Coptic church grew and grew. (Copt is an ancient name for Egyptian.) Soon almost all Egyptians were Christians and they were sending out missionaries to North Africa and even to Europe.

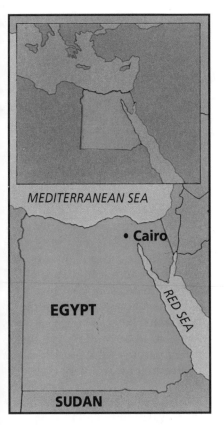

MEDITERRANEAN SEA

• Cairo

EGYPT

RED SEA

SUDAN

In AD 642 Egypt was invaded by Arab Muslims. Christians were forced to become Muslims, and thousands were persecuted and martyred; but the Coptic church never completely disappeared. Egypt became a Muslim country. It still is.

Today there are about nine million Coptic Christians living in this Muslim land. Only the President can give them permission to build a new church, to repair or even paint their old one. Needless to say, the President doesn't often give such permission! Christians are not allowed to tell others about Jesus and his love for them. Some still find ways of helping people and witnessing for Jesus.

## Teaching the poor

Farouk and Ali are two Christians from the Coptic Evangelical Church. Most days they go to the village where Fuad and Ramzi live. 'Why do you go there?' a friend asked them. 'Aren't you afraid you'll get sick from all the rubbish?'

'In the Bible,' they replied, 'we read that God cares for the poor and needy. God wants us to care for them, too, and that's why we go to the village. They need help because they have so little. Our church is helping them as much as it can. We have set up a clinic so that they can get help when they're ill. We have a little school, and we're teaching the children to read. Come with us and meet some of the children.'

As soon as Fuad and Ramzi saw Farouk and his friends, they rushed over to them. Soon scores of chattering, ragged children surrounded the visitors. 'It's time for our reading lesson,' Farouk told them. 'Go and get your books.' Fuad and Ramzi and some of the other children ran to their little huts and returned with their carefully wrapped books, eager to learn.

'We have a church here, too,' Ali told their friend. 'Every Saturday and

## You Can Pray for Egypt

### Dear Lord Jesus

1 Give Christians the courage to witness to Muslims even though they know they can be punished for doing so.

2 May your Holy Spirit give Christians a great love for you as they study your word. Call many to serve you as pastors.

3 Show the government that it's unfair to prevent Christians from building or repairing their churches without permission from the president.

4 Help the people in the slums and rubbish dump villages to know how much you care for them, because Christians care for them and help them.

5 Thank you for all the work among children and young people. As they learn about you in Sunday schools, youth clubs and summer camps, make them excited about following you.

6 May many people go into the Christian bookshops in Egypt to buy Bibles and Christian books.

7 Please use the Jesus film and the Christian radio programmes in Arabic to speak to many people.

Sunday the church is full. These people are discovering that, even though they are so poor, they are important to God. Psalm 113 verse 7 tells us, "(The Lord) raises the poor from the dust and lifts the needy from the ash heap." That's what we're seeing happen here but we need people to help us.'

# EQUATORIAL GUINEA

## FROM RICHES TO POVERTY

Equatorial Guinea is a small West African country with two provinces. The first is the fertile island of Bioko and another tiny island about 370 miles to the south west, called Pagalu. The second province, Rio Muni, is on the African mainland.

Thirty years ago Equatorial Guinea was one of the richest countries in West Africa. It had large cacao plantations producing the best cocoa in the world, and exported coffee and timber to Europe. Today Equatorial Guinea is one of the poorest countries in Africa.

### The work of an evil man

'How poor our country is!' said Federico's father.

'Why is that?' Federico asked.

'We were once ruled by Spain,' his father replied, 'but when Spain gave us independence a man named Macias Nguema became President. He was cruel. He put many people in prison, where they were often tortured and killed. He closed schools and churches, and we couldn't buy food. Hospitals ran out of medicine.

'Thousands of Nigerians used to work in the cacao plantations, but they became scared and returned to Nigeria. That meant there was no one to work on the plantations. Boys as young as seven had to do military training, or their parents were punished. The President was a very evil man.'

'What else happened?' Federico asked. 'What happened to the churches? I'm glad I can go to church and learn about God. Macias Nguema is dead now, isn't he?'

'Yes, he is,' his father replied. 'Macias Nguema forced all the missionaries and Catholic priests to leave our country. He didn't believe in God, and wanted us to become an atheist country. He wouldn't even allow parents to give their children Christian names! He forced all the Protestant churches to become part of one organization. Some of the church leaders thought political power was more important than teaching people about the power of God. Only a few remained really true to God.'

In 1979, after a *coup d'état*, Macias Nguema was arrested, tried and shot. His nephew, Colonel Teodoro Obiang Nguema Mbasogo, became President in his place. He asked Spain and other countries in Europe to help his sad and needy country. Everyone hoped the new President would bring new hope to their country.

## Come back and teach us!

As soon as they were allowed to send letters, Christians wrote to former missionaries. 'Please come back and teach us,' they begged. When missionaries returned for a visit, they found some of the Christians had stood firm for Jesus. Jesus had helped them through the difficult times, even though some of them had been in prison. Several more years passed before missionaries were allowed to live there again. They found many people wanting to learn about God.

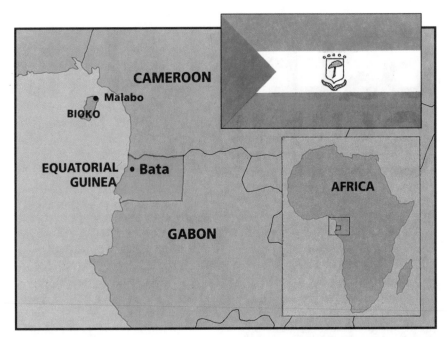

# We want to follow Jesus!

One day a missionary, with an evangelistic team, was driving through a small village. A man ran out in front of their Landrover waving his arms. 'Stop! Stop!' he shouted. 'We want to know how we can follow Jesus.'

The team stopped and explained the Way of Salvation to the people in the village. Three of them decided to follow Jesus and ask him to be their Saviour.

At Bible club a missionary asked a sad-faced little girl why she was crying. 'My baby brother became sick and died,' Regina sobbed. 'My mother is crying all the time. I loved him so much, and always looked after him when our mother went to market. What happens when someone dies?'

The missionary gently explained that the Lord Jesus loved that little boy and took him to be with him in heaven. Regina listened carefully. The next week Regina asked a lot more questions and the missionary showed her the answers from the Bible.

Because Equatorial Guinea is a Catholic country, many children know about Jesus, but they do not learn that Jesus forgives their sins and gives new life to those who trust him. Very soon Regina asked the Lord Jesus to come into her life, and told her brothers and sisters.

Missionaries are doing all they can to help the people. They are providing medical centres, clubs for children and Bible Schools. Although Equatorial Guinea is still a poor land, people are finding that Jesus loves them, helps and gives them hope.

## DO YOU KNOW?

Equatorial Guinea is the only country in Africa where Spanish is the official language.

## You Can Pray for Equatorial Guinea

### Dear Lord Jesus

1 Please may Equatorial Guinea have a government which will lead the country wisely.

2 Help people to know that only you can give new life and real hope for the future.

3 Please forgive those pastors who were not true to you. May they repent and become your true servants.

4 Call more men who love you to be pastors in the churches.

5 Be with those who are studying in Bible School and help them to learn how they can bring others to know you.

6 May the children who go to Bible Clubs learn how much you can help them and that you want them to trust you always.

7 Please send more missionaries to teach people how much you care for them.

# GREENLAND

## THE LARGEST ISLAND IN THE WORLD

### An Eskimo boy

Eight-year-old Sigssuk was excited. He had been on his first seal-hunting trip with his father and they had caught two seals. He felt as though he had been preparing for this special day all his life. Sigssuk is an Eskimo, or Inuit, and lives with his family on the north-west coast of Greenland.

As soon as he could walk, Sigssuk was given a puppy and a toy whip, so that he could learn to train his own dog. His father had built Sigssuk a special kayak and hung it from a beam in the house so that it was just a few inches from the ground. There little Sigssuk sat, learning how to control the canoe with a small paddle. Every summer, when it is daylight all the time, he had gone with his family on camping trips. It was great fun learning to catch little auks in a net as they whirred around his head. What a feast they had that day as they ate some of these little birds. The rest of the birds were put in a special sack made from sealskin to be kept for food in the winter months.

During the long, dark winter months, when the sun never rises, Sigssuk goes to the village primary school. There he learns to read and write, but he also has lessons from some of the older men about hunting. They even show the boys how to build their own kayaks and sledges.

In winter the weather is often too bad for Sigssuk and his friends to play out of doors.

Instead, they stay in their snug houses and listen to the grown-ups telling stories about their hunting expeditions. The children like to play at arm-wrestling and try their skill at 'cat's cradle' with a piece of string.

Greenland is the largest island in the world, and most of it lies inside the Arctic Circle. There are so many bays and fiords that the coastline is almost as long as the distance round the earth at the Equator! Nearly all of Greenland is covered by a huge ice sheet which no one can live on. Most Greenlanders live in small towns and villages on the south and west coasts, where they can go fishing and hunting.

## The first Christians

Greenland was first discovered by Erik the Red, a Norseman from Iceland, about 1000 years ago. 'Come back with me to Greenland,' he urged his family and friends in Iceland. A group of brave men, women and children made the dangerous sea journey back to Greenland with Erik. They took with them all their horses, cows and sheep. His son, Leif the Lucky, became a Christian on a visit to Norway. When he returned to Greenland he told everyone about Jesus and many people, including his mother, became Christians.

In 1721 a missionary arrived from Denmark, hoping to find Christian descendants of those first settlers. He didn't find any. Soon other settlers came from Denmark and Norway. Gradually people started to become Christians and were baptized. They built churches in almost every little town and village, and the Bible was translated into the Greenlandic language.

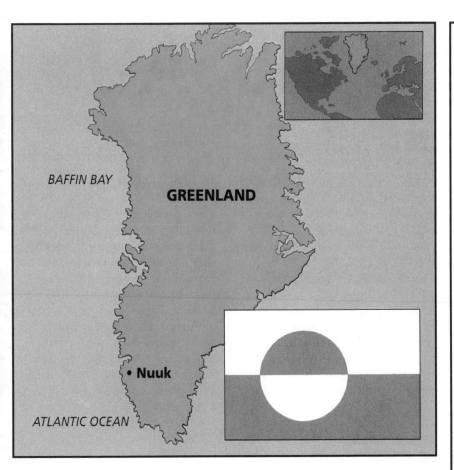

BAFFIN BAY

GREENLAND

• Nuuk

ATLANTIC OCEAN

## You Can Pray for Greenland

### Dear Lord Jesus

1 Please use the camps to help many children and young people come to know you as their Saviour.

2 Help missionaries to teach new believers clearly from your Word.

3 Show the people of Greenland that being a Christian means more than going to church. Help them to understand that you can forgive their sins and can keep them from sinning.

4 Help new believers to make Christian friends, so that they can encourage one another to follow you.

5 Teach young Christian couples to be true to you, so that their children will grow up knowing your love and care.

6 As Christians read the new translation of the Bible, may they be challenged to follow you with their whole heart.

7 May your Holy Spirit bring new life to many in Greenland.

## Ancestors and charms

Olaf lives in Nuuk, the capital of Greenland. At Christmas time, like many Greenlanders, he and his family go to church. Olaf calls himself a Christian, but he still does not realize that Jesus died for him, and that Jesus can be his special friend. When he fell and broke his arm, his mother stitched a charm on his parka to keep him safe, and asked wisdom from the spirits of her ancestors. This is animism, not Christianity.

Now several evangelical Missions are working in some of the towns. They organize special meetings and camps for children and young people, and meetings for adults. Niels became a Christian at one of these camps. When he went home, he found it very hard to live a real Christian life because all his friends drank and took drugs. It's certainly not easy to be different from everyone else! Even some of those who go to short-term Bible

Schools and Discipleship Training Courses find it hard to keep growing as Christians once they return to their homes.

Jesus said about himself, 'If the Son sets you free, you will be free indeed' (John 8:36). Many people in Greenland who say they are Christians need to know that Jesus can set them free from sin and give them the power to live pure lives for him.

# GUINEA-BISSAU

## JESUS SETS US FREE!

### A birthday

Even churches have birthdays! In 1990 the Evangelical Church in Guinea-Bissau celebrated its 50th birthday. How excited everyone was. The Central Church in Bissau, the capital city of this small West African country, was packed. With hearts full of joy, the choir sang and people spoke about God's love and care for them. It was a great event!

In 1940 Bessie, a young English missionary, arrived in Guinea-Bissau. Bessie loved to tell people about Jesus. She invited everyone she met to come to church in her living room. Soon men, women, boys and girls were asking Jesus to forgive their sins. Jesus changed them so completely that they wanted others to know what he had done for them. So the church grew and spread, and more missionaries arrived to help the young church.

In those days the country was called Portuguese Guinea, because it was ruled by Portugal. The people wanted to be free, so they fought the Portuguese in a very long war. Portuguese is still the official language but many people speak only Creole or their own tribal language. Most people are very poor. They have to work very hard to get enough food to eat. Only a few children go to school and learn to read and write.

### Books and Bibles

The Christians of Guinea-Bissau want to learn what God says in the Bible, so the missionaries help them all they can. What a task for them! First of all they have to learn Portuguese, then Creole, Balanta, Papel or another language. Then they have to make simple books and charts. The children are quick to learn, but the parents often find it really hard. Some of the Christians go to Bible School, where they learn to teach others to follow Jesus.

But what were the Christians going to read? They didn't have Bibles or even New Testaments. The missionaries and some of the other Christians started the long task of translating the New Testament into several of the languages spoken in Guinea-Bissau. Often it is very difficult to find exactly the right word to use. How can you find a word for mountain in a country where there are no mountains? The language-helper gave the translator a word which he thought described a mountain. She found it meant a mound about two metres high made by small, white insects called termites. Can you imagine Jesus going up a termite hill to pray?

## Many languages

Although Guinea-Bissau is a small country, there are more than 25 tribes living there and each tribe speaks its own language. Some Balanta and Papel Christians are already witnessing to them, but many more evangelists are needed because there are so many tribes.

The people of Guinea-Bissau wanted to be free from the power of Portuguese rule, but it is much more important for them to know that Jesus can set them free from the power of evil spirits and make them new people.

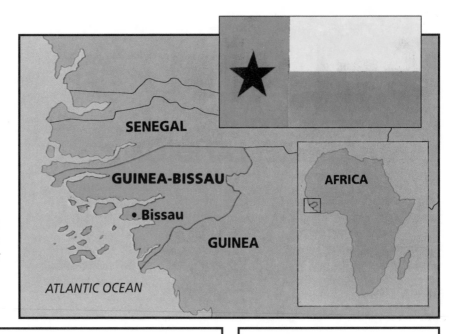

# Jesus loves twins

Most people in Guinea-Bissau are afraid of evil spirits. Apili and her twin brother Okanz listened eagerly as granny recalled what happened when they were born. 'Your mummy died,' she said. 'Because you are twins the witch-doctor said that one of you must be a baby sent by the spirits and had killed her. No one would pick you up or feed you. We were all afraid. The witch-doctor said you should both be left outside to die.'

'But, granny, you didn't leave us to die, did you?' asked Okanz.

'No,' granny replied, 'I couldn't bear to hear you crying all the time, so I hid you in a basket and took you to the ladies who tell us about Jesus. What could I do with two weak, tiny babies?'

'It isn't true about one of us being a spirit baby, is it?' Apili asked.

'No, my child. The ladies explained that God loves you both and wants us to look after you because you are special to him. They showed me how to mix milk for you in a bottle, and then prayed to Jesus for us. At first my family were very angry, because they thought the spirit baby would harm them. When nothing bad happened they did not mind so much. Soon I wanted to follow Jesus, because I realized he is more powerful than all the evil spirits.'

'So now we are all walking the Jesus way,' said Okanz, happily. 'We are not afraid of the spirits.'

## You Can Pray for Guinea-Bissau

### Dear Lord Jesus

1 Please help those who are translating the Bible into Balanta, Papel and Creole to find the right words to use.

2 Give patience to those who are teaching the Christians to read.

3 May your Holy Spirit help Christians understand what they read in the Bible.

4 Help students in Bible school to learn more about you, so they can teach others.

5 There are so many tribes who are afraid of evil spirits. May they soon hear the Good News that you can set them free from all their fears.

6 As people listen to the gospel radio broadcast every Sunday evening, may they want to know more about you.

7 Please use the 'Jesus film' to bring many to know you.

## DO YOU KNOW?

Only the Balanta, Bijago, Mandingo and Papel tribes have the New Testament in their own language, but the New Testament has also been translated into Creole, the trade language of the country.

# ICELAND

## LAND OF FIRE, LAND OF ICE

'Tell me a story,' Erik pleaded as he curled up on the couch by the side of his father. 'Tell me how Iceland became a Christian country.' His father smiled. He loved to tell this story.

In winter, Iceland is dark almost all the time, but the people enjoy reading, telling stories and playing games such as chess. Erik is glad his home is comfortable and warm. Like most of the houses in Reykjavik (pronounced *Raik-ya-vik*), the capital of Iceland, it is centrally heated by the hundreds of hot springs there.

### Choosing Christ

'It all started a very long time ago,' Erik's father began, 'when the first settlers came to Iceland. They were great adventurers and made long and dangerous journeys across the sea. Some came from Norway seeking a new life. Others were Vikings who had settled in the British Isles and married Christian women. Soon almost half the people in Iceland were Christians, but there were many who still wanted to follow the old Norse gods like Thor and Odin.

'In the year AD 1000 our

## Glaciers and volcanoes

Iceland is often called the land of fire and ice. Huge glaciers and icesheets cover large areas of the land. There are so many active volcanoes that the ground is black with volcanic ash and rocks. In 1963 a fisherman was amazed to see the sea boiling while he was out fishing. A few weeks later the top of a volcano poked out of the sea and was soon shooting steam, fire and ash high into the air. In a very short time the volcano became the new island of Surtsey.

Ten years later, early in the morning when everyone was still asleep, a volcano erupted on another island. The people all managed to escape to the mainland. When the volcano died down, they returned to the island. They discovered that most of the buildings had been destroyed and the ruins covered with thick black ash. Only the gate to the cemetery was unharmed. On the gate were the words, 'I am the resurrection and the life,' a reminder that they should thank God for their miraculous escape.

Today, most people in Iceland say they are Christians, and many recite the Lord's prayer every day. Sadly, few go to church anymore. The large churches in Reykjavik are almost empty. Some people want to go back to the old Norse religion. Many others worship elves, dwarves and trolls which, they believe, have their homes in hills and trees on the island.

## DO YOU KNOW?

Iceland's parliament, the '*Althing*', is the oldest parliament in the world.

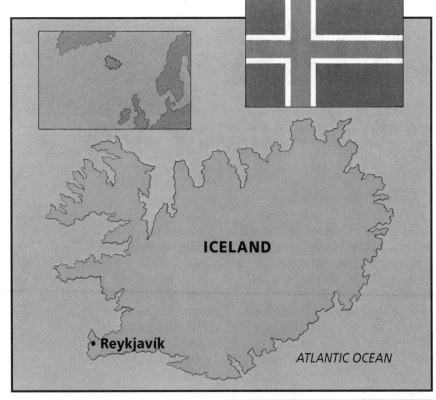

ICELAND

• Reykjavík

*ATLANTIC OCEAN*

ancestors met together in the Althing, our National Assembly, to decide whether we should continue to follow the old gods or become a Christian country. They elected one highly respected man to decide for everyone, and he chose to follow Christ! For almost a thousand years, from that day to this, Iceland has been a Christian country. It became the custom, in nearly every home, for the family to meet together each evening to pray and read the Bible.'

Iceland is a large island, about 500 miles north of Scotland. The early settlers were farmers and fishermen, who had to work extremely hard to provide food for themselves and their families. Although they were often hungry, they made up their minds they would never be defeated by the difficult land they lived in.

## Revival needed!

In the summer Erik goes to a Christian camp, where he hears more about the Lord Jesus who wants to be with him to help him day by day. Each year the Gideons* give a New Testament to each 10-year-old child and newly-qualified nurse. Erik's

brother is studying at university. He is excited because other students are discovering that knowing Jesus changes their lives completely.

In the year 2000 Iceland will celebrate 1000 years of Christianity. Those who truly love the Lord Jesus are praying that before then there will be revival in Iceland and many people will become real Christians.

*The Gideons is an international organization that places free Bibles in hotels, schools, hospitals and prisons. In some countries they give a New Testament to every 10-year-old child.

## You Can Pray for Iceland

### Dear Lord Jesus

1 May many Icelanders discover that Christianity is more than just a part of Icelandic tradition, and that they need to know you for themselves.

2 May Christians learn to overcome the powers of the old Norse gods, and elves, dwarves and trolls, in the name of Jesus.

3 Help students in Bible School to learn from your Word and become faithful pastors, evangelists and witnesses for you.

4 Thank you for every university student who knows you. Help them to keep true to you, even when their friends are not interested in knowing you.

5 Use the Christian camps, so that many boys and girls will choose to follow you.

6 May each child and student nurse read the New Testament given them by the Gideons.

7 Use the celebrations in AD 2000 of a thousand years of Christianity to bring revival to the church in Iceland.

# INDIA

## LAND OF A MILLION GODS

### Festival

'Wake up!' Sanjay shook his brother. 'The *sadhus* (holy men) have already smeared ash on themselves and have started to go down to the river. It's time for us to be on the move, too. It will soon be dawn.'

A week earlier Sanjay and his brother had left their village in Uttar Pradesh to make the long journey for the *Mela* (festival) at the holy place where the great Ganges and Jamuna Rivers meet. Sometimes they'd managed to get a ride on a bullock cart. Once or twice they'd travelled on crowded buses piled high with people's belongings and goods

for sale in the markets. Mostly they'd walked along the hot and dusty roads.

They'd spent the last two nights huddled together by the side of a small dung fire waiting, with countless other pilgrims, for this very moment. Sanjay stretched himself. All around him were tents and people, millions of people, there for the Maha Kumbh Mela.

'Come on,' he urged his brother. Soon they were caught up in the vast crowd of people, pushing, slipping, sliding,

dodging sacred cows and wandering goats, on their way down to the river. At last they reached the mighty river and stepped into its muddy, dirty water. With his face to the rising sun, Sanjay poured water over himself, hoping, like countless other Hindu pilgrims, that his sins would be washed away by the water's flow.

The Maha Kumbh Mela is one of India's great religious festivals and is held every twelve years. Hindus, whether they are high caste or low caste, come from all over India, hoping to wash away their sins in the Ganges. The sins they want to wash away have little to do with breaking God's laws or hurting other people. The sins they are concerned with are touching things they believe are unclean and failing to keep their caste rules. Most of them have never heard that only Jesus can give them truly clean hearts and lives.

# A million gods

Indians are very religious. Some are Muslims, but most are Hindus. Others are Christians, Sikhs, Buddhists or Jains, and still more are animists. Often there has been fighting between the different groups and many people have died.

Wherever you go in India, you will find temples and shrines where people worship. Do you know there are said to be more than a million Hindu gods? Some, like Brahma the Creator of the World, Vishnu the Preserver, and Shiva the Destroyer, are very important. Every day the Hindu priest has to wake up the gods in his temple, bathe them with milk and honey, offer them food and pray to them.

When people come to worship at a temple, they bring offerings of food or flowers for the brightly painted gods. They ring the temple bell to make sure the god or goddess is awake. Even when they have made their offerings and prayed, they are never sure the god will be kind to them. How different are these gods from the God we know who is always watching over us, caring for us.

Christian missionaries have worked in India for hundreds of years. One of the best known is William Carey, who went to India more than 200 years ago. He was sure that God

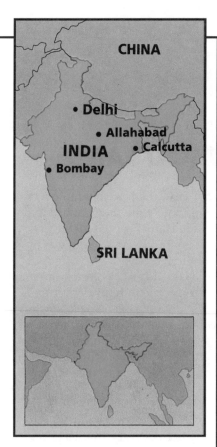

wanted everyone, everywhere, to learn about his great love. He lived there for almost forty years and translated the Bible into several Indian languages and taught many people to follow Jesus.

Although missionaries have preached the gospel, helped the poor, looked after children and cared for the sick, only a small number of Indians really know and love Jesus. Many Hindus despise Christians because most have come from communities known as *outcastes* or *Harijans*. It is hard to be a Christian when you are despised and persecuted for your faith. Will you pray that God will help them to follow Jesus whatever the cost?

It is difficult to get a visa to be a missionary in India now, but many Christians and Indian missionaries witness faithfully for the Lord Jesus. There are millions in India who still need to hear the Good News that only Jesus can save them from their sins. Not one of their million gods that have 'ears that cannot hear and eyes that cannot see' can ever do that.

## DO YOU KNOW?

By A.D. 2020 it is expected that there will be more people living in India than in any other country in the world. There are 4,635 people groups in India, and 1,652 different languages are spoken.

## You Can Pray for India

### Dear Lord Jesus

1 Please show many Indians that keeping their caste rules and offering gifts to their gods can never give them true peace or hope.

2 May your Holy Spirit show Indian Christians that caste does not matter to you and that you love them and died for them all.

3 Be with Indian missionaries who go to other parts of India to tell people about you. Help them to learn the languages of the people so they can share the gospel clearly.

4 Call many Christians to help the millions of people who live in the huge cities of India, especially those who are homeless and very poor.

5 Use the millions of Scripture portions, New Testaments and tracts that are given out each year to bring grown ups and children to know you.

6 As people listen to Christian radio programmes, help them to understand that you alone can wash them clean from all their sins.

7 Send more Christians from countries like our own to work in India and to show the people there just how much you love them.

# IRAQ

## DO YOU KNOW?

Two out of every three children in Iraq believe they will not grow up to become adults.

## A SAD AND TROUBLED LAND

Iraq is a large Arab republic in the Middle East. Almost three-quarters of the people living in Iraq are Arabs, but in the northern mountain region many of the people are Kurds.

### A Bible land

In the Old Testament we often read about people and events in the land we now call Iraq. God called Abraham to leave Ur, the city-state where he lived, and go to a place God would show him. In the days when it was known as Assyria, God sent the prophet Jonah to preach in Nineveh in the north of the country. After the Babylonians had conquered all that area, the Jewish people were taken into exile there, and this is where Daniel served Nebuchadnezzar and Belshazzar, kings of Babylon.

On the day of Pentecost there were people in Jerusalem from Mesopotamia, as Iraq was then called. They took the Good News of Jesus back to their own country. There are still Christians in this Muslim country today.

### Wars

During the second half of the twentieth century Iraq has been a sad and troubled country. In July 1958 the king and prime minister were killed during a violent revolution, and a military government took their place. There were several coups d'état, and in July 1979 Saddam Hussein came to power. There has been no lasting peace in the land.

Iraq wanted to control the Shatt-al-Arab waterway to the Persian Gulf, and for eight years fought a terrible war against Iran. Millions of Iraqi and Iranian people were killed, but it was a war that no-one really won.

In the north cruel attempts were made to get rid of the Kurds. Many were killed and their homes razed to the ground. All round the world people watched their television screens with horror, as they saw the pictures of columns of homeless Kurdish refugees trudging hopelessly across snow-covered mountains away from the ruins of their villages.

## The Good News of Jesus

When 'Desert Storm', the Gulf War, started, the evangelical church in Baghdad decided to meet each day for prayer. 'Our family and friends went down into the nearest shelter to pray and read the Scriptures together,' Yousef recalls. 'Sometimes Muslims came to listen, and some of them became Christians. We can often share our faith. On Christmas Day, in 1991, the Jesus film was shown on Iraqi television, so millions of people were able to hear the Good News of Jesus.'

Yousef smiled. 'Only thirty years ago,' he said, 'Christians were persecuted in this country. Now that has changed, and many people want to hear the gospel. I never thought that I would see our church so full or that we would see a film like this on television.'

He picked up his Bible. 'Praise God for the people who pray for us, and for those who brought Bibles into Iraq!' he said. 'Now the government has given permission for Arabic Bibles and Christian children's books to be published in Baghdad.

'But we are poor,' he added, 'and it is hard for us to earn enough money to feed our families. It is harder still for us to help our churches to send young people to Bible School to train as leaders. Please never forget to pray for us,' he pleaded.

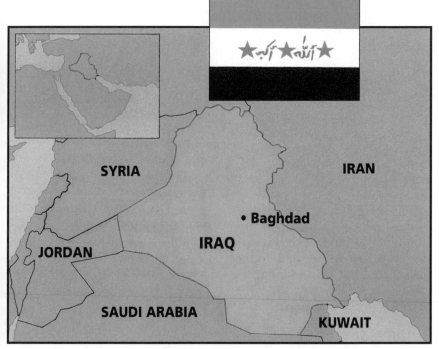

## Suffering

'Why should we suffer so much?' a sad-faced doctor asked. 'In our hospital we have so little medicine and our equipment is worn out. We understand why other countries are trying to prevent us from selling the oil our country produces, and why they are stopping supplies coming into Iraq. They are determined that our government will never again be able to form a strong army, but ordinary people are suffering. We cannot treat the people who come to us for help, and there is not enough food for the children.'

Yes, at the end of the twentieth century, Iraq is a sad and troubled land, but exciting things are happening there, too.

Far away in the south of the country, where the great Tigris and Euphrates rivers meet, the Marsh Arabs were driven out of the swamps which have been their home for hundreds of years. Many of them died, and few have been able to continue their ancient way of life.

In 1991 Iraq invaded the neighbouring country of Kuwait. Many countries, including Britain and the U.S.A., took part in the short, but terrible, Gulf War. Once more, Iraq was not truly defeated.

## You Can Pray for Iraq

### Dear Lord Jesus

1 As people in Iraq suffer, help them to discover that you are a friend who cares for them and helps them when life is difficult.

2 Use the Jesus film to help many to understand that you came from heaven to earth to show them the way to God.

3 Help true Christians to follow you faithfully. May your Holy Spirit always give them courage to tell others about you.

4 May there soon be enough Bibles for everyone who wants one. Help each person who has one to read it, and so learn more about your truth.

5 May the churches in Iraq reach out to help groups like the Marsh Arabs who know nothing about you.

6 Thank you for the radio broadcasts in Arabic and Kurdish. As people listen to them, help them to open their hearts to you.

7 May there soon be a government in Iraq which will lead the country wisely towards peace and not to war.

# ISRAEL

## THE HOLY LAND OF JEWS, CHRISTIANS AND MUSLIMS

### The Promised Land

'Tell me about our nation,' Tanya pleaded. 'Why did we come to Israel? You told me we should have a much better life here because this is the homeland of the Jews.' Tanya's family are Messianic (Christian) Jews who emigrated from Russia.

'It's a long story,' Tanya's father replied, 'which goes back thousands of years. This is the "Promised Land" God gave to his people, the Hebrews, and it was here that men such as David and Solomon lived. Jesus was born, and lived and died here, too, so it is special to Christians. Muslims believe that Mohammed travelled from Jerusalem to heaven on his winged horse to speak with God. It's no wonder it's called "the Holy Land" by Jews, Christians and Muslims!

'In the 2nd century A.D. the Romans drove most of the Jews out of the land. They settled in almost every country on earth. We call this the *Diaspora*, or scattering. Wherever they went, the Jews were persecuted. In their hearts they prayed and longed for the day when they could return to their own land.

### Conquered

'The Arabs conquered Palestine in AD 634. There were still some Jews living here, but most people were Arab Muslims. In the last hundred years or so, more and more Jews have returned to Palestine, but it was not really our land. In 1922 Britain was asked to govern the country. It split the country in two. The eastern part was put under Arab rule, and Jews were allowed to settle in the west.'

### A new state

'But that wasn't the real beginning of Israel, was it?' Tanya asked.

'No,' her father continued. 'In 1948 the United Nations voted to split the western part of the country into two States, one Jewish and the other, Arab. There was a lot of fighting and the British left.

On May 14th, 1948, the new Jewish State of Israel was formed. Ever since there have been wars and a lot of fighting between Jews and Arabs. Thousands of Arabs have had to leave their homes. They are still looking for a state of their own. It's sad we cannot all learn to live together in peace.'

'Where have all the immigrants come from?' Tanya wanted to know. 'We came from Russia, and some in my class at school came from Ethiopia.'

'Many of the first Jews who came to the new State of Israel had suffered badly in Central Europe during World War II. Terrible things were done to them, and they wanted a homeland of their own,' Tanya's dad told her.

'Since then we have come from many countries around the world. We have all tried to make our country a success, but it is difficult because there is not enough work. I was a doctor in Russia, but there are already too many doctors here.'

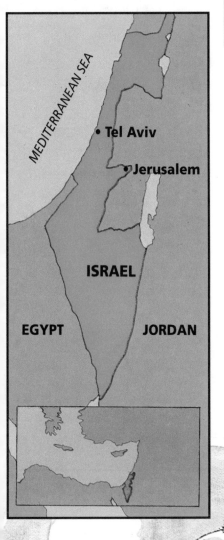

## Christians

'Some of the children at school make fun of me and say unkind things about me. They say I can't be a Jew because I'm a Christian,' Tanya said. 'Why?'

'Here in Israel,' her dad said, 'there's a popular song which tells of the deep longing of the Jews for the Messiah to come and bring peace to his people. They do not understand that Yeshua (Jesus) is the Messiah God promised long ago.

'All the way through the Old Testament we read God's promise of a Saviour. They are still looking for him to come, but we know Yeshua is the One God tells us about. More and more Jews are discovering this for themselves. Some Jews feel we can no longer be Jews if we trust in Yeshua, because they do not understand that he is the Messiah.'

'Aren't some of the Arabs living in Israel Christians too?' Tanya asked. 'We've only Jewish Christians in our church.'

'There are whole villages of Arab Christians, but we don't often meet them,.' her father replied. 'A friend of mine told me that some members of his church visited an Arab church recently. It was a big step for them to take, because the Jews and Arabs are enemies. He said they were kind, and made them feel at home. I was reminded of the words in Galatians 3:28 which says we "are all one in Christ Jesus".

'We must pray that many people in our country, Jews and Arabs, will come to know Jesus, and that he will help us to be friends with one another.'

## You Can Pray for Israel

### Dear Lord Jesus

1 May many Arabs and Jews in Israel come to know you as the true Messiah and turn to you for forgiveness.

2 Help Messianic (Christian) Jews and Arab Christians to trust each other, and to know they are all part of your great family.

3 May both Israeli and Arab Christian parents help their children to love you and be faithful to you.

4 Please help the translators of the Bible into modern Hebrew for children to find the right words so that children will understand your Word.

5 Help those who are writing Christian books, magazines and Sabbath School materials to make them attractive and easy to understand.

6 When tourists visit Israel may they not only visit historic places, but help them to pray that Christian Jews and Arabs will always be true to you.

7 Please bring peace to the Middle East, especially between Palestinians and Israelis.

# MADAGASCAR

## WHERE CHRISTIANS WERE MARTYRED FOR THEIR FAITH

Like most of her people, Queen Ranavalona I of Madagascar believed in the power of charms and idols and worshipped the spirits of dead kings and queens. During her coronation ceremony in 1828 she took two idols in her hands. She said, 'I have received you from my ancestors; I put my trust in you; therefore support me.'

Ten years earlier two brave Welshmen arrived in Madagascar. They were both sure God had called them to serve him there. Each had his wife and young baby with him. In a very few months only David Jones was still alive, and even he was weak and ill. His wife and baby, his friend and his family had all died. How easy it would have been for him to have gone home to Wales and forgotten about the people of Madagascar. David Jones did not give up because he knew God wanted the people of Madagascar to hear about Jesus.

### School without books

At that time King Ramada I ruled in Madagascar. He never became a Christian, but he knew that the missionaries would help his people. David Jones started a little school and the king's son was one of his first pupils. It must have been a very strange school because Malagasy, the language of Madagascar, had never been written down. This meant there were no books. Soon other workers joined David Jones and they started writing down the language. Now the pupils could be taught to read and write

and more and more children started going to school.

David Jones and his friends taught the grown-ups to read and write as well, and to learn other useful things such as carpentry, weaving and printing. Even more important, they started to translate the Bible into Malagasy. They worked very hard, especially after King Ramada died, because they knew it was important that the new Christians should have God's Word in their own language.

Diégo Suarez

Majunga

**MADAGASCAR**

Antananarivo

INDIAN OCEAN

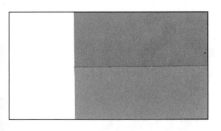

## Martyrs for Jesus

When Ranavalona became queen she was afraid she would lose her power because so many people were becoming Christians. Instead of worshipping idols and the spirits of their dead kings and queens, they wanted to be true followers of Jesus. The queen became very angry and told the people of Madagascar that anyone who dared to worship or pray to the God of the missionaries would be put to death.

Many of the Christians defied the queen and met in secret, in homes, caves or on mountain-tops, to pray and read the Bible. Thousands of Christians were tortured and put to death because they would not stop following Jesus. The wicked queen just could not get rid of the Christians. Instead, more and more people started to follow Jesus, and when Queen Ranavalona died in 1861 there were far more Christians than when she had started her cruel reign.

You would think that Madagascar should still be a Christian country, but people forget so quickly all that God has done for them. Do you remember the story in the Bible about Moses leading the people of Israel out of Egypt? How they grumbled, even though God helped them day after day! Even when they reached the Promised Land they soon forgot the ways in which God had helped them and started to follow other gods. Sadly, this has also happened in Madagascar.

### DO YOU KNOW?

In 1835 at the start of the persecution, 70 copies of the first translation of the Malagasy Bible were buried. The Christians used these Bibles in their secret meetings.

## Whose power?

An old, crippled man showed a visitor a sacred place where there were three shrines. 'A powerful Malagasy king struck this rock and water came out of it,' he said. 'This is a place of healing. Then he put his stick into the ground and two trees sprung up. They help us to contact the ancestors.'

'Do you believe in the power of this shrine?' the visitor asked.

'I have been healed through drinking the water from this spring,' the old man replied, 'but I am a Christian and I go to church every week.'

'Who healed you?' he was asked. 'Was it the spirit of the king, or was it God?'

The old man smiled. 'I thank them both. They are the same.'

More than half the people of Madagascar say they are Christians, but many are like this old man and try to keep the old ways of worshipping idols and the spirits of the dead as well as being Christians. It doesn't work. They need to know that Jesus wants them to follow him and love him with all their heart and soul and mind, just as the Malagasy martyrs did more than a hundred years ago.

## You Can Pray for Madagascar

### Dear Lord Jesus

1 Thank you for missionaries working in Madagascar. Help them to teach the Malagasy Christians to follow only you.

2 Remind the people of Madagascar of the testimony of the Christians who were martyred and help them to be faithful to you.

3 Show them that you are greater than all the idols and that they can trust you completely.

4 Bless the work of Scripture Union and the International Fellowship of Evangelical Students among students in schools and colleges.

5 Help young people who become Christians to keep true to you and to tell others that you can make them into new people.

6 Use Christian radio programmes to reach many people with the Good News of Jesus, especially in places it is difficult to reach.

7 Thank you for the Malagasy Bible. May its message come alive to Christians today, just as it did when Queen Ranavalona was persecuting Christians for following you.

# THE MALDIVES

## BEAUTIFUL ISLANDS – BUT NO CHRISTIANS

### Holiday paradise

Dad pulled a world atlas from the bookshelf and opened it at a map of India. 'Look, Peter,' he said, pointing to a chain of tiny islands in the Indian Ocean. 'These are the Maldives. I thought we could go there on holiday this year. They're about 400 miles south-west of the southern tip of India and stretch for about 500 miles, right down to the equator.'

Peter's dad handed him a travel magazine. 'See for yourself how beautiful they are.'

'Wow!' exclaimed Peter. 'Coral islands! Coconut trees! Look at those sandy beaches! The islands look as though they are floating in the sea.' Peter started to read the magazine. 'It says that the sea will be warm. We're going to have great fun swimming, scuba diving and snorkelling. It's going to be a fabulous holiday.'

Every year thousands of holidaymakers, like Peter and his family, visit the beautiful Maldives to bask in the sun and swim in the clear blue waters. They stay in hotels specially built for tourists and often the only Maldivians they meet are those who work in the hotels.

'I think we should find out all we can about the Maldives before we go,' dad suggested. 'We'll see what it says in *Operation World* and we'll find out more in books about India.'

### 1,200 islands

'Do you know, dad,' Peter said a few nights later, 'there are 1,200 little islands in the Maldives, but only 202 have people living on them? The islands are very flat: usually they reach no more than two metres above sea level. Sometimes they are completely flooded in tropical storms.

'The capital island of Malé is small. It must be very crowded, because 60,000 people live there!

The International Airport is on Malé, but most of the tourist hotels have been built on their own islands. I guess we'll have to go by boat to our hotel.'

'Well done,' his dad replied, 'and I've found out a few things, too. The people call themselves *Divehi*, which simply means "islanders". Their language is

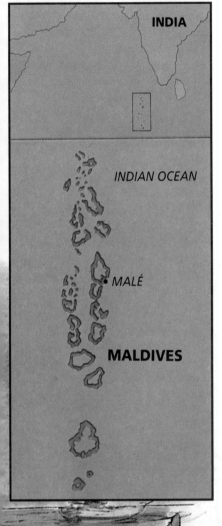

INDIA

INDIAN OCEAN

MALÉ

MALDIVES

called *Divehi*, too, and is written from right to left. Nearly every child goes to school and learns to read and write, and in Malé there are schools where the children study in English. If they want to go to college or university they have to go to another country.'

'What do most Maldivians do?' Peter asked. 'With so much sea they must be fishermen!'

'Boat building is important, and more than a third of the people are fishermen,' dad replied. 'Many Maldivians are poor, in fact some people say the Maldives are among the twenty poorest countries in the world. They must be very glad of the money they earn from tourists.'

'Have you found anything out about their religion, dad? What do they believe?'

### Afraid

'Someone at church gave me a little book,' dad answered. 'It says the Maldivians are Muslims, but they're also afraid of *jinns,* or evil spirits. The Maldivians build their homes without windows so that the *jinns* cannot get in. Some of the older houses even have a low wall across the doorway to keep the *jinns* out. The fishermen are scared of evil spirit monsters in the sea. Many people are so afraid of evil spirits that they will not go out after dark. They often wear a blue glass charm around their necks to keep them from harm.'

Peter shivered. 'That sounds quite scary. I hope the *jinns* won't get us! Aren't there any Christians there?'

'No, there are no Christians, and missionaries are not allowed

to work there,' dad replied, sadly. 'Sometimes Christians from other countries go there to work, but they are forbidden to speak about Jesus. I have even read that a Christian tourist had his Bible taken from him. We don't have to be afraid of evil spirits because Jesus is more powerful than they are. Do you remember what we read in church on Sunday in Luke 4:31-36? Jesus will look after us and keep us from harm.'

'Well, dad, we could start doing something now! Jesus can change the world,' Peter exclaimed. 'We can start praying right now that the people of the Maldives will hear the good news that Jesus saves! I think our holiday is going to be much more exciting than just swimming and sunshine!'

## You Can Pray for the Maldives

### Dear Lord Jesus

1 Challenge many Christians around the world to pray that the power and fear of evil spirits in the Maldives will be broken.

2 Work in the hearts of the leaders of the country so that they will allow Christians from other countries to share their faith with Maldivians.

3 May Christians who work in the Maldives shine for you, even though they are forbidden to speak about you.

4 As Maldivians study in other countries, may they find you as their Saviour, and return to tell their families of the joy and peace you give.

5 Help Christian missionaries in sea ports around the world to find ways of telling Maldivian sailors about you.

6 May the way Christian tourists behave on holiday attract Maldivians to you.

7 May the Bible soon be translated into Divehi.

# NEW CALEDONIA

## A PART OF FRANCE IN THE PACIFIC OCEAN

### New ways and old

'What do you learn at school?' grumbled Pierre's father. 'Each time you come home to the village you seem to have forgotten more of our Kanak ways. You don't know how to make copra from the coconuts, and you can't even remember how to break open a coconut. You can't help build a village house or even work on the farm. What do you know about our way of healing, or of the work of the *totem* (spirit) of our clan?' Pierre looked round his father's small, thatched house. He could not help comparing it with the houses in Nouméa, the capital,

where he went to school. There large houses built of cement and high-rise apartment blocks line the streets. He thought about all the goods on sale in the super-markets. It was all so different from his father's village.

'I'll be able to get a job in Nouméa or in one of the nickel mining companies,' Pierre replied. 'But you will have to teach me how Kanaks live, because I want to help our people. Like you, I want our country to belong to us and not to France.'

'Once it was our land,' Pierre's father reminded him, 'but when the French settlers came they took the best land to grow rice and

coffee. Later, when they discovered nickel, they took more of the land away from us. Our people fought for the land, but the settlers were too strong. They brought illnesses with them and many of our people died. Now there are more people from other countries in New Caledonia than there are Kanaks.'

'There's a lot of talk in Nouméa about 1998, when we hope we shall be able to vote for indepen-dence from France,' Pierre added. 'Many of the Catholics in Nouméa don't want indepen-dence. I wonder what it will mean for us if we do become an independent country?'

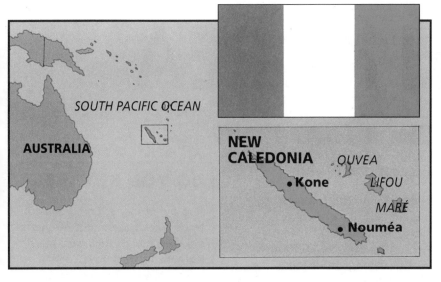

## DO YOU KNOW?

Although New Caledonia is only 250 miles long and 30 miles wide, it is the world's second largest producer of nickel.

## A prison colony

New Caledonia is a group of islands about 750 miles east of Australia, in the south-west part of the Pacific, in an area called Melanesia. Melanesia means 'the black islands'. It earned its name because the people have dark skins and woolly black hair.

In 1774 Captain James Cook landed on the main island. The tall pine trees and hills reminded him of his home, far away in Scotland, so he named it New Caledonia. Caledonia is the Latin name for Scotland.

About 60 years later a Christian from the island of Tonga, hundreds of miles across the Pacific Ocean to the east, arrived in New Caledonia. He began to preach the gospel. After a few years the London Missionary Society sent two Christians from Samoa* to help teach the people about Jesus.

*See YCCW Vol.1 page 98

## Good News

The French claimed New Caledonia in 1853 and for more than thirty years used it as a prison colony. They shipped thousands and thousands of convicts from France to live and work on the islands. Many of their descendants still live there. Catholic priests came from France to look after the French settlers. Now people from many other countries have gone there to work in the nickel mining industry.

When missionaries arrived from England, one of their first tasks was to translate the Bible into the main Kanak language. Although French is now the official language, forty other languages are spoken there. That is a great many languages in a country where there are only 178,000 people. Wycliffe Bible Translators are translating the Bible into some of these languages.

Almost every town and village in New Caledonia has either a Catholic church or a Protestant church. Nearly every Kanak wants to keep the ways of the *totem*, but also claims to be a Christian.

Does this mean we don't need to pray for the people of New Caledonia?

In Nouméa few Europeans go to church except for special services. There are about 6,000 Muslims from Java and the Middle East working in New Caledonia. Not many of them know that God sent Jesus to set them free from the power of sin. The Kanaks want their country to be free from French rule. Far more than that, they need to know the power of God in their lives which can truly set them free.

## You Can Pray for New Caledonia

### Dear Lord Jesus

1 Please show wealthy people in Nouméa that true happiness can come only through knowing you.

2 Make rich people see that they should help those whose land was taken from them, and who are poor and suffer as a result.

3 May your Holy Spirit help pastors to teach your Word clearly so that everyone can understand it.

4 When old Kanak customs are linked with evil spirits please give Christians the strength to obey you and to speak out against them.

5 Please send revival to the church in New Caledonia so that each Christian will want to live in a way that pleases you.

6 Help national Christians and workers from WBT as they translate the Bible into some of the languages spoken in New Caledonia.

7 As people in New Caledonia prepare to vote for, or against, independence in 1998, please keep them from fighting one another.

# NORTH KOREA

## FORCED TO FOLLOW A GOD-KING

### A first god-king

Hwanung, the son of the great creator, says a Korean legend, decided to come down from heaven and become king of everything he could see. As he gazed around at the beautiful country he heard a bear praying, 'Make me into a human being. I'm tired of being a bear.'

Feeling sad, Hwanung told the bear to take twenty pieces of garlic and some mugwort (a plant with a bitter taste) and stay in a cave for a hundred days. The bear obeyed, and turned into a woman!

The woman longed for a son. She gave birth to Tangun. According to the legend, Tangun was the first king of Korea. He reigned for more than a thousand years and his people worshipped him.

### A second god-king

Not long ago there was another man who thought he was a god-king like Tangun. In 1945, when Korea was divided at the end of World War II, Kim Il Sung, the 'Great Leader', came to power in North Korea.

At that time there were many Christians in North Korea, including 400,000 Protestant believers. In fact, there were so many Christians in Pyongyang, the capital city, that it was often called the 'Jerusalem of Korea'.

Kim Il Sung expected everyone, even the Christians, to worship him. He made everyone wear a

### DO YOU KNOW?

Two out of every three people in North Korea are under 30 years old. This means that most North Koreans have always been taught to worship their god-king. Only one person in six is old enough to remember what life was like before North Korea became a communist country.

badge with his picture on it. Every building in Pyongyang had to have his picture above the doorway. All over the city brightly coloured posters showed Kim Il Sung speaking to thousands of people. And high on a hill outside the city, he built a 100-metre high statue of himself with his arms outstretched, smiling down on the city.

RUSSIA

CHINA

NORTH KOREA

Pyongyang

SOUTH KOREA

JAPAN

PACIFIC OCEAN

## No other god

The 'Great Leader' did not want his people to worship anyone else. He was a communist, and was determined to get rid of every trace of religion in North Korea. All the church buildings were destroyed. Nearly three million Koreans were killed. Among them were thousands of Christians.

At school the teachers showed the children a little black book. They asked, 'Are there any books like this hidden in your house? Search for them, even in your parents' bedroom, then tell us.' Some children discovered that little black book and told their teachers. They never saw their parents again. The little black book was the Korean Bible.

Some brave people continued to follow Jesus and met in secret to worship him. Two million people fled to South Korea, but Kim Il Sung attacked the South, too. Everyone was afraid. Korea was no longer like its name 'Chosun', the Land of Morning Calm.

Instead of learning to sing praises to Jesus, the children were taught to worship Kim Il Sung. They sang, 'He is our Great Leader and we keep his image in our hearts.'

'Welcome to Heaven,' tourist guides greeted visitors to North Korea. 'You are now in the earthly paradise of our Great Leader Kim Il Sung.' Kim Il Sung made himself like a god.

## Death of the god-king

In 1994 Kim Il Sung died. The people wept and mourned because the one who had made himself their god was dead. He had already trained his son, Kim Jong Il, the Dear Leader, to take his place.

Very few people ever see Kim Jong Il. Some say he is ill, and others say that he prefers to watch what happens on television cameras. Ordinary people are beginning to complain because they are so poor and because there are so many things they are not allowed to do. Will Kim Jong Il have sufficient power to rule the country? There are others who would like to seize that power for themselves.

## The one true God

People all round the world have been troubled in their hearts for North Korea. Christians have tried all sorts of ways to tell the people about God's love for them. They've beamed in radio programmes, although most radios in North Korea can receive only government broadcasts. They've even sent Christian literature to North Korea by balloon, and in plastic envelopes which they've thrown into the sea.

In South Korea many Christians are praying that the North Koreans will see that they've been worshipping a false god. They are waiting for the time when they can go there to encourage the Christians, and tell others about the true God. Will you pray with them?

## You Can Pray for North Korea

### Dear Lord Jesus

1 Help Christians in North Korea to be brave enough to worship only you. Help them not be afraid of those who would try to harm them.

2 May every Christian stay on your side, even when other people betray them because they follow you.

3 Please may Christians in North Korea be allowed to tell others about you.

4 Thank you that Korean Christians who live in China can visit North Korea. Help them to witness to their relatives and encourage Christians.

5 May everyone who has a radio which is not tuned to the government programme listen to Christian radio programmes.

6 Use every piece of Christian literature that reaches North Korea to speak to someone there about your love and care.

7 Please help South Korean Christians and others around the world to keep on praying until North Korea is once more open for the gospel.

43

# REPUBLIC OF GUINEA

## WHERE MISSIONARIES WERE BANNED

### The Sacred Forest

'Your son no longer belongs to the Sacred Forest!' the leader of the evangelistic team explained. 'Now he is a Christian he belongs to Jesus. He is free to follow Jesus so I cannot make him obey you.'

The village chief was very angry and afraid. The people of his village belong to the Sacred Forest cult. Many of them say they have been 'born again' through the devil's mouth! When the devil, or leader of the cult, comes into the village, everyone is supposed to hide indoors.

The chief's son had become a Christian and refused to do this any longer. He knew that if he hid when the devil came, he would be denying that God had set him free from the devil's power.

The people of the forest region of Guinea in West Africa are animists. They are afraid of the devil and evil spirits. Only when they have courage to turn their backs on animism and trust in Jesus will they be free from the devil's power. Some of the forest people have become Christians. They are joyfully telling their friends that Jesus sets them free!

### Missionaries go home!

Most other people living in Guinea are Muslims. When Guinea was under French rule, missionaries worked there, but very few people became Christians. After Independence the president wanted Guinea to be a Communist country as well as a Muslim one.

In 1967 the missionaries were made to leave. Only a few from the Christian and Missionary Alliance were allowed to stay. Their hearts ached as they prayed for the millions of people in Guinea who had never heard about the God who loves them.

God answered their prayers. In 1984 the president died and missionaries were allowed to return to Guinea. Even before that, God was at work. Guinea had become a poor country. Men wanted money so they could buy food and clothes for their families. They travelled to other African countries to earn money. Sometimes they found Jesus.

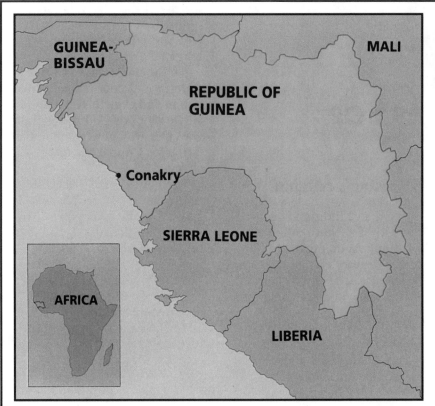

GUINEA-BISSAU

MALI

REPUBLIC OF GUINEA

• Conakry

AFRICA

SIERRA LEONE

LIBERIA

Alhaji did not give up. He knew that God would give him courage to speak about Jesus, and to help the people in his village all he could. Now eight men have trusted in Jesus.

Like Alhaji, other people have come to know Jesus and are witnessing for him in Guinea. They want their people to know that Jesus is the Son of God and loves them and wants them to belong to him. Only Jesus gives peace and salvation. Neither trying to keep the laws of Islam nor belonging to the devil can ever do that!

# New life in Jesus

Alhaji was a Muslim. He wanted to know more about God, so he prayed, fasted and studied the Koran. He needed money, so he left Guinea and went to Gambia. He quickly found work, sewing for some missionaries. They gave him a book, but it was in English.

He learned to read English because he really wanted to know what the book said! It told him about Jesus, the Son of God. One day the missionaries gave him a Bible. As Alhaji read it, he started asking questions. 'Who wrote the Bible, and who wrote the Koran? The Koran says that the God who sent Mohammed created heaven and earth, and the Bible says the God who sent Jesus created them. Which book was written first?'

One day as Alhaji started his Muslim prayers he asked God to show him the truth. As he prayed 'May God bless Mohammed,' he

suddenly thought, 'Hasn't Mohammed got God's blessing yet?' Soon he realized that the Bible is the true Word of God and he became a Christian.

When Alhaji told his wife she was angry. She left him and returned to Guinea. That was very hard for him, but he did not stop studying the Bible, or following Jesus or praying for his wife. God worked a miracle! Alhaji's wife became a Christian and went back to live with him. They felt sure they should return to Guinea to tell their people about the God of the Bible who loves them all.

## God loves the people of Guinea

When they reached their home village everyone welcomed them. The imam (the leader of the mosque) asked Alhaji to speak at the mosque. Alhaji told the people about God's love. He set up a little tailor's shop and started to teach five young men to make clothes. Those five young men became Christians, but when their families persecuted them, they became Muslims again.

## You Can Pray for Guinea

### Dear Lord Jesus

1 Please help the Christians to show others that you love them and want them to follow you.

2 Help men like Alhaji to tell others that you can set them free from fear.

3 Call more missionaries to serve you in Guinea and help those who are teaching Christians to become pastors and evangelists.

4 May the forest people understand that worshipping spirits and the devil will only bring them fear, but you can give them peace and joy.

5 Help Muslims to understand that they can find God only by trusting in you, and not by trying to obey all the Muslim laws.

6 Use cassettes with Christian messages to help animists and Muslims turn to you.

7 May many young people learn to follow you, even though others make fun of them and try to make them turn back to their old ways.

# RUSSIA

## A THOUSAND YEARS OF CHRISTIANITY

### Christ is Risen!

'Christ is risen!' The priest's clear voice rang out in the crowded church. 'He is risen indeed!' the triumphant Easter response rose from the lips of the congregation. Olga glanced at her grandmother, whose wrinkled face shone with joy. She was pleased that her grandmother found so much happiness in church. After all, life was difficult for her as her pension was so small.

As they left the church, with its golden, onion-shaped domes, Olga turned to her grandmother. 'I am so glad we can go to church to worship God,' she said. 'Tell me again what it was like when churches were closed and it was against the law for children to learn Bible stories.'

'Let's sit on the park bench, for it's a long story. After standing in church, I shall be glad to rest,' grandmother smiled.

### Choosing a religion

'More than a thousand years ago there lived a Prince called Vladimir. At that time the people of this country worshipped many different gods. Prince Vladimir was convinced that these gods were false.

'He wanted our country to follow a great religion, and decided to find out all he could about Judaism, Islam and Christianity. There's a legend which says that in A.D. 988 Prince Vladimir saw a light shining over

the city of Kiev. He was sure this bright light came from Christ, who was telling him which religion he must choose.

'So Russia became a Christian country, and poor peasants, rich nobles and even the Czar himself all worshipped God in the same way. Our way of worship in the Orthodox Church has never changed.

'Then in 1917 the Bolsheviks drove the ruler, Czar Nicholas II and his family from power. The Bolsheviks demanded change because, although some people were very rich, most Russians were very poor. Under a man called Lenin they seized the government and took control of all the farms and factories. They turned Russia into a Communist country. For many of us life became even harder than before.'

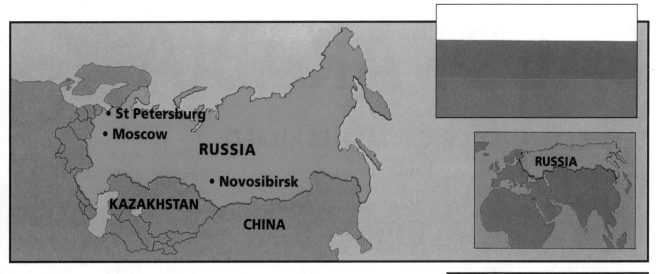

## Religion banned

'What happened to the church?' asked Olga.

'Religion was banned and only a few people had Bibles,' grandmother replied. 'Most churches were closed. I used to weep when I passed our beautiful church, because it had been turned into a cow-shed. Then I remembered that our Saviour was born in a stable.

'We did not want to stop worshipping God. The government allowed a few churches to stay open, but they were closely watched by the *KGB* (secret police). Many Baptists and others formed "underground" churches. They met in secret, often out of doors. They knew they would be punished if they were caught.

'They were very careful but the *KGB* often found them and took away their pastors. Some were tortured and put in prison, or were sent far away to Siberia. The Communists made life very hard for Christians and punished many of them, but they just couldn't get rid of Christianity.'

'I am glad it's different now.' Olga looked up at her grandmother and smiled. 'I enjoy our lessons about the Bible at day school and at Sunday school, and I like going to church. How did this all change?'

## A new day

'In 1985 Mikhail Gorbachev was elected as General Secretary of the Communist Party. He knew many things were wrong in our country and started to make changes. He lifted the ban on worship and started to give us back the church buildings the government had taken from us.

'In 1988 Christian leaders from around the world were invited to Russia to celebrate a thousand years of Christianity in our country! Since then we have been free to worship God again and children like you can learn about him. Yes, Christ is risen indeed!'

'Sometimes Christians from other countries come to our school and teach us Bible stories,' Olga told her grandmother. 'They say that all round the world people have prayed for us. We know God has heard their prayers.'

'Yes, Olga,' grandmother said, 'and we must go on praying. Many Russians still know little of the Bible. All sorts of cults and religions have come into our country. They want our people to follow them. We need people who can teach us so that we can follow the living Jesus and be true to him.'

## DO YOU KNOW?

Russia is the world's largest country. It is so huge that at 6 a.m. in Moscow it is already 5 p.m. in the far east of the country.

## You Can Pray for Russia

### Dear Lord Jesus

1 Thank you for Russians who stayed true to you, even though many were put in prison and tortured because they were Christians.

2 Thank you that Christians can worship you now. Please keep them from listening to cults and other religions which would take them away from you.

3 May your Holy Spirit help all Christians shine for you in this land where there is still so much fear, deceit, greed and unemployment.

4 Use Christian television and radio programmes to reach many people with the Good News about Jesus.

5 May every Christian soon have a Bible which they will read and study eagerly.

6 Bless the work of Bible schools and colleges as they train pastors and leaders to teach the people who are turning to you.

7 May there be leaders in Russia who will lead this great country and its millions of people justly and wisely.

# SAUDI ARABIA

## THE BIRTHPLACE OF MOHAMMED

### Pilgrimage

'The time of the *Hajj* (pilgrimage) is drawing near,' Hassan told his twelve-year-old son Abdul. 'This year you and I will go on pilgrimage together.' Hassan and Abdul live in Riyadh, the royal capital of Saudi Arabia.

'I know the *Hajj* is one of the five pillars of Islam,' Abdul replied, 'and that every Muslim is expected to go on pilgrimage to Mecca, the birthplace of Mohammed, at least once in his lifetime. Tell me what happens.'

'I've already been three times! Last year more than two million pilgrims came from countries all round the world. What a brotherhood we have!' Hassan exclaimed. 'We all wear identical white clothes to show we are all equal in the sight of Allah. After our ritual washing and prayer we go to the *Kaaba* and walk round it seven times keeping it on our left. As we walk round it we have to try to kiss the Black Stone or at least touch it.'

'The *Kaaba* is very old, isn't it? The Koran tells us it was built by Abraham at the place where Allah provided water for Hagar and Ishmael, doesn't it?' Abdul asked.

'Yes,' his father replied, 'and when Allah told Mohammed that all Muslims should worship towards Mecca, Mohammed cleared all the idols from the *Kaaba* and made it a holy place. Every year a new black silk cover is put over it.

'When we have walked round the *Kaaba* seven times we have to run seven times between two sacred pillars, praying all the time. The next day we go to the Plain of Arafat, about ten miles outside Mecca. We must remember to take our radios with us so we can hear the sermon.

'Afterwards we collect small pebbles and throw them at three stone pillars to get rid of the evil that is inside us. On our way home we'll visit the Tomb of Mohammed in Medina.'

## The keeper of Islam

Mohammed wanted the whole of Arabia to follow Islam. Shortly after his death in A.D. 672 every Christian and Jew was turned out of Arabia. Today Islam is the only religion allowed in the country, because the government considers itself the keeper of Islam. The religious police make sure that women dress according to the law and that all the shops close when the call for prayer booms out. They hunt out anyone they think is not obeying the strict Islamic laws.

# An oil-rich desert land

The Kingdom of Saudi Arabia is a hot, dry, desert country covering most of the Arabian Peninsula. The nomadic tribes who lived there were brought together by a strong Arab leader who was declared king in 1926. So the new kingdom of Saudi Arabia was born. The king's word is law, and every part of the country's life is controlled by the large royal family.

When oil was discovered, Saudi Arabia became powerful and wealthy. Countries all round the world wanted to buy their oil. Some of the money from oil has been used to build better houses, schools and universities and to develop industries. The Saudi Arabian government sends huge sums of money to Muslim organizations around the world to help them to publish Muslim literature, train Muslim missionaries and build huge mosques.

### Guest workers

Does that mean there are no Christians in Saudi Arabia? No! There are a few brave Saudi Christians, who know they run the risk of death if they are discovered. Thousands of people from other countries go to work in Saudi Arabia. Some work in oil companies, but many, from countries such as India, South Korea and the Philippines, work as labourers, housemaids and nurses. There are Christians among them.

In 1990 some Filipinos were given permission to hold an open air evangelistic service for other Filipinos. 'It was a great time,' Maria said. 'About 3,000 Filipinos came. At the end of the meeting hundreds of people came forward, to show they wanted to follow Jesus.

'The religious police arrived and ordered the preacher to send the people home. Instead, the preacher prayed for those policemen and told us all to bless them! We knew the police could beat us and have our leaders put in prison or sent back home, but God worked a miracle, and those policemen left!'

Where do you think the last pilgrimage, from this life to the next, will take the Saudis? Will you pray that many of them will find that Jesus alone is 'the way, the truth and the life'?

## You Can Pray for Saudi Arabia

### Dear Lord Jesus

1 Please look after the Christian guest workers and keep them from being frightened of the religious police.

2 Show guest workers how to share their faith, and protect them from the prying eyes of those who would harm them.

3 Work in the hearts of the authorities so that they will allow foreigners to hold Christian meetings.

4 The few Saudi Christians often feel very lonely. May they meet other Arab Christians who will encourage them to follow you.

5 May your Holy Spirit teach the Saudi believers to grow and be strong in you.

6 When Saudis go to other countries to work or study, may Christians invite them to their homes and show them what it really means to be one of your true followers.

7 May the ban on Christian books and Bibles be lifted so that anyone who wants a Christian book or Bible may have one without fear of being punished.

# SPAIN

## A LAND OF CONTRASTS

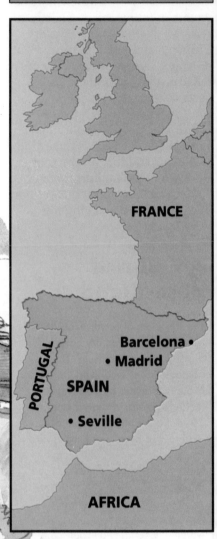

### A street meeting

'Come on,' José shouted to his friends. 'The Evangelicals are starting their open-air meeting.' They threaded their way between the sidewalk cafés and the crowds who were enjoying their evening stroll and gossip. They could see a group of people around the entrance to the busy underground station and hear singing and guitars being played.

José and his friends pushed and wriggled their way to the front. They wanted to make sure they wouldn't miss the story. 'I hope it will be about one of the people Jesus healed, just like he healed your brother Juan!' panted Carlos.

The sunny country of Spain lies in the south-west corner of Europe. It is a land of fairy-tale castles, soaring church steeples, colourful fiestas and delicious food. If you stand on the south coast on a clear day and look across the shimmering Mediterranean Sea, you can see the coast of North Africa. It's no wonder many people think of holidays when they think of Spain!

### A big problem

Madrid, where José and Carlos live, is the capital of Spain and is right in the centre of the country. More and more people are moving from the countryside into Madrid and to other towns and cities. Many are poor and tired of farming. They think it will be easy to get work in the city, but often there are no jobs for them, and they have to live in very small, crowded flats.

When José and his family came to live in Madrid, they stopped going to the Catholic church because they said they no longer believed in God. They had no work, no faith, and soon José's brothers were stealing and taking drugs. 'What else is there to do?' they said.

One of José's brothers died and another, Juan, became ill because they had been taking drugs. 'Who will help us?' their anxious parents wondered. 'No-one seems to care, and we feel so alone.'

## Help

One night they stopped at an open-air meeting. 'Why are you so unhappy?' a young man asked them. When they told him he replied, 'I know where your son can get help. Would he come to the Betel Centre?'

God worked a miracle in Juan's life. He was looked after, and as he got better he started to work at the Centre. He learnt that Jesus has the power to heal and to free even drug addicts from the sins that grip them so tightly. He learnt that Jesus is not a dead figure on a cross. He has risen from the dead and is alive today, and gives new life to all who trust in him.

But it is not only drug addicts who need to know that Jesus saves.

## DO YOU KNOW?

**In his letter to the Romans, Paul wrote that he planned to visit Spain, a Roman colony. Many Jewish people lived there, and he wanted them to hear the Good News about Jesus.**

## A Feast Day

Although Spain is a Catholic country, many people now go to church only on special occasions.

Lidia was excited. Today was the feast day of the village saint. Everyone had been busy, cleaning the village street and preparing the feast. Her sister, Maria, who worked in Madrid, had come home specially.

As the church bells rang, Lidia and her family made their way to the church for Mass. 'Can it be true,' she wondered as she looked at the statue of Jesus on the Cross, 'that the bread really becomes Jesus' body? But I must not ask questions. Mary,

Mother of God, please help me.'

Soon the solemn service was over. Outside the church the band struck up a familiar tune. The young men pulled the floats carrying the gilded statues of their saint and one of Jesus. Soon everyone joined in the procession. It didn't take long for Lidia to forget her questions as she and her friends joined in the excitement, feasting and dancing!

In more than 7,000 towns and villages across Spain, millions of men, women and children do not realize that Jesus is alive today. Is there something you can do to help them know him?

## You Can Pray for Spain

### Dear Lord Jesus

1. Help churches to make open-air meetings so interesting that many people will stop to listen to the gospel message.

2. May every one who accepts a gospel tract or leaflet come to know you.

3. Please use the work of centres like Betel to show drug addicts that you have the power to help them stop taking drugs.

4. Thank you that there is now freedom to preach the gospel in Spain. Help Christians to find many ways in which they can tell others about you.

5. May your Holy Spirit fill each Christian believer with such a love for yourself that they will be bold in telling others about the many wonderful things you want to do for them.

6. May many people listen to Christian radio programmes which will tell them the true way of how to be forgiven.

7. Thank you for the many Spanish Gypsies who have come to know you as Saviour. May your Holy Spirit help them to share the Good News of Jesus with their brothers and sisters.

# SYRIA

## WHERE PAUL WAS CONVERTED

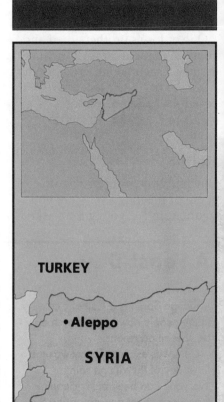

### Changed lives

'You've become a Christian! What do you mean, Ibrahim?' demanded Maria. 'Our family have always been Christians and we belong to a church here in Damascus. There have been Christians here since New Testament times.'

'Yes, Maria, that's true.' replied Ibrahim. 'Some of the first Christians lived right here in Damascus. It was an important place even then, and travellers and traders came from far and wide. In Bible times Saul came here to persecute the Christians, because he was determined to stop the Christian faith being spread to other places. Instead, God spoke to him before he reached Damascus and Saul ended up a Christian.

'When I went away from home to study in Aleppo, Maria, I met other Christians. They were excited about their faith and told me that Jesus could be my own special friend. They taught me to study the Bible. What a wonderful book it is! Reading the Bible has helped me to know Jesus for myself. Would you like to come to a Bible study group with me? My friends have a video, too, of the life of Jesus. It's really good.'

### An ancient land

Damascus, the capital of modern Syria, is an ancient city. In fact it is thought to be the oldest continuously inhabited city in the whole world! It is even mentioned in Genesis, the very first book in the Bible. There, too, you can read about the River Euphrates, which still flows through Syria (Genesis 2:14).

Syria has been a secular country since 1973, but three-quarters of the people are Sunni Muslims. There are other Muslim sects in the country, and the present rulers belong to a smaller Muslim group called the Alawites.

In most towns and cities in Syria there are Christians who belong to the Orthodox and Armenian Churches. They are highly respected in the country, and many have good jobs as merchants, teachers, doctors and lawyers. Others work for the government and in the armed forces. Many of them go to church every week, but few of them really know Jesus for themselves.

Christians have a lot of freedom in Syria. No one stops them from going to church, and at Christmas and Easter there are Christian programmes on both radio and television. People can buy Bibles from the two Bible Society bookrooms and are free to watch the Jesus film.

Wonderfully, hundreds of people like Ibrahim and Maria are coming to know Jesus for themselves. Both in the new Protestant churches and in the older churches people are keen to study the Bible. Many are finding new life in Jesus.

## A divided city

What about the Muslims? For almost 1300 years Muslims and Christians have lived in Syria, but they don't have much to do with each other. At the present time missionaries are not allowed to live in Syria, and there are not enough full-time Christian workers. How then will the Muslims hear the gospel?

'We live in the Christian part of Damascus,' explains Ibrahim, 'and the Muslims live in their part. We don't understand one another. The name "Islam" means submission, and we think of Islam as a harsh religion. Muslims don't understand us, either, so it is very difficult for us to talk with them about our faith.

'I have one or two Muslim friends. I try to witness to them by the way I live. I want them to see that Jesus has made my life pure and clean, and fills me with joy. Some of my Christian friends do not understand why I want my Muslim friends to know Jesus, and my Muslim friends are afraid they will be persecuted if they become Christians. Jesus says "I am the way, the truth and the life." I want all my friends and family to know that, too.'

## DO YOU KNOW?

Some Syrian Christian merchants were very upset when they had to vacate their shops near the Ummayad Mosque in Damascus while that part of the city was being modernised. They believe that when Jesus returns to earth, he will land on the minaret of that mosque, and they want to be near at hand when he comes.

## You Can Pray for Syria

### Dear Lord Jesus

1 Thank you that Syrian Christians are free to meet together to worship you. Help them to rediscover the excitement the first Christians had in following you.

2 May those who trust in you help others who call themselves Christians to know you as their very own friend.

3 Help Christians to live in a way that will show Muslims and other people they meet every day what you are really like.

4 Use the Bible study groups meeting in churches to help Christians grow.

5 Thank you for the work of the Bible Society bookrooms. May reading the Bible change many lives.

6 May many people watch the Arabic video of the Jesus film and come to follow you as a result.

7 Bring peace to Syria and the neighbouring countries of Lebanon and Israel.

# TRINIDAD

## CARNIVAL AND CALYPSO

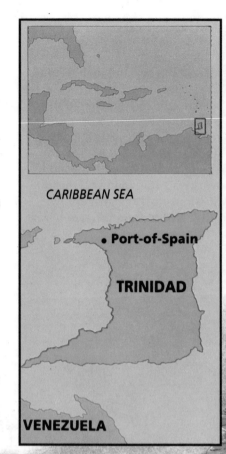

CARIBBEAN SEA

• Port-of-Spain

TRINIDAD

VENEZUELA

### Carnival

Carnival! The streets of Port-of-Spain, the capital of Trinidad, throb to the rhythmic beat of steel drums. It is Shrove Tuesday, or Mardi Gras, the final day of Carnival. Thousands of men, women and children wearing elaborate fancy dress throng the streets, glittering and sparkling as they dance to the exciting music. They have spent weeks preparing to play mas, or masquerade, creating fantastic costumes, practising music and writing witty *calypso* songs. At midnight the festivities come to an end, for the next day is Ash Wednesday, the start of Lent.

### Festivals

Trinidad is a land of festivals. In November they celebrate *Divali* (pronounced Dee-wa-li), the Hindu festival of lights. Candles shine from hundreds of thousands of little clay pots, while people spend the night feasting and dancing.

Another Hindu festival, *Phagwa,* or New Year, takes place in March. There's great excitement and an air of carnival as bands of dancers on the streets are pelted with red food dye.

Muslims have their festivals, too. On *Hosay* they remember the murder of two warrior brothers, Hosein and Hassan. They carry models of Hosein's tomb through the streets, to the beat of drums and chanting. They hold great feasts and spend the night dancing. The next day they throw the 'tombs' into the sea as a sign of burial.

### Many faiths

Nine-year-old Earl sat outside his home with Winston, his father. He was excited and tired after Carnival. 'It's fun living here, isn't it, dad?' he said. 'But why do we have so many festivals? Why do people who look so different from each other all call themselves Trinidadians?'

'It's true,' his father replied. 'We are an amazing mix of people. Most of us have our roots in Africa, India and Europe, but some come from the Middle East, China and South America. There are Christians, Hindus and Muslims, because they all

## DO YOU KNOW?

In the south of Trinidad there is a lake of pitch (tar). A local legend says the lake was formed when a chief killed a sacred hummingbird, making the gods so angry that they drowned his whole village in pitch.

brought their own religion and culture with them. It all began a long while ago!

'Christopher Columbus discovered this island in 1498. As he sailed near the south-east coast he saw three mountain peaks which reminded him of the Holy Trinity. So he named the island Trinidad.

'It became a lonely and neglected outpost of Spain until the eighteenth century, when Catholic refugees from French colonies settled here. They developed sugar and cacao plantations and brought slaves from Africa to work for them. They tried to force the slaves to forget their African religions and become Catholics. In 1797 Trinidad was captured by the British and became a British colony.

'In 1834 slavery was abolished, but the plantation owners still needed workers. They brought people from India, promising them that, after they had worked on the plantations for five years, they could have a free journey home. Many chose to stay in Trinidad and were given small plots of land for themselves.

Some of the Indian workers were Muslims, but most were Hindus. They have kept their own religion and culture, but all Trinidadians like to join in *Carnival, Divali* and *Hosay.* Our National Anthem reminds us that "here every race and creed find an equal place".'

Trinidad, the most southerly of all the Caribbean islands, is separated from the South American country of Venezuela by only 11 kilometres of sea. Sugar, cacao, oil and pitch once made it a wealthy country. Now many people are unemployed

and poor. There is an increase in crime, drugs, child abuse and tensions between the different races and religions.

Every Sunday Earl and his family go to an evangelical church. Earl enjoys singing, and the people of Trinidad really know how to sing! Some Christians visit the schools to teach the children about Jesus. This is important for, although more than half the people of Trinidad say they are Christians, many of them do not really know Jesus.

Will you pray that all the Christians will come to love Jesus so much that they will want to tell their Hindu and Muslim friends about him? What a day of rejoicing there will be in heaven when Trinidadians of every race turn to Jesus!

## You Can Pray for Trinidad

### Dear Lord Jesus

1 Give the Prime Minister and the government wisdom as they try to help people of different backgrounds to live happily together.

2 Thank you for all the Hindus who have become Christians. Help them to share their faith with other Hindus.

3 Help Christians to find more joy in telling others about you than they do in their festivals.

4 As children learn more about you in school and church, help them to become your true followers.

5 Thank you for Christian radio and TV programmes. Please use the messages to teach people how they can live lives that please you.

6 Bring many people into the Christian Literature Crusade bookshops to buy and read Christian books.

7 May your Holy Spirit give the church a great desire to tell Muslims in Trinidad of your love for them.

# URUGUAY

## WHERE CHRISTMAS DAY IS CALLED 'FAMILY DAY'

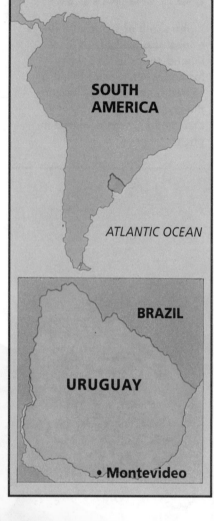

### Family Day

Uruguay, the smallest country in South America, is sandwiched between the two huge countries of Brazil and Argentina. Beautiful white beaches and a pleasant climate attract tourists from other South American countries and from Europe.

Although sheep and cattle thrive on the rolling, grassy plains and low hills, more and more people are moving away from the countryside. Everyone in Uruguay goes to school, and many study at university. They are sure they will be able to earn more money in one of the towns than they would as farmers.

Most Uruguayans are descendants of settlers from Spain and Italy. Early in the twentieth century they turned their backs on Roman Catholicism. Even Christmas Day lost its name and is now called 'Family Day'. For many people God ceased to exist. They became agnostics.

When people don't believe in God there is an empty place in their lives. Uruguayans thought that a good education, good wages and a good pension were far more important than God, but they are finding they were wrong. These things can never fill that empty place.

In Montevideo, and in almost every town, there are Christian churches. Pastors and Christians want to share their faith, and talk to their friends about Jesus. They hold special meetings, but, at present, only a few people are becoming Christians. So many other religions want to attract the Uruguayans.

## God answers prayer

Twelve-year-old Gonzalo was curious when some Christians held a tent campaign near his home. As he listened to the evangelist, Gonzalo knew that he had to ask Jesus to save him from his sins. For the next two years he went to a young people's club called 'Royal Ambassadors'. He was keen to learn all he could about God, Jesus and the Bible.

Gonzalo's father belonged to a group who practised a kind of witchcraft called *Macumbas*. One day his father started to shout at him. 'You're not to go to church any more!' Gonzalo decided he ought to obey his father, even though he did not want to. The boys in the club prayed for Gonzalo. Three weeks later his father changed his mind. The boys were all excited because God had answered their prayers so quickly.

## Birthday parties

Christians are wanting to share their faith with others. Ana is a student at Montevideo University. She wondered how she could she tell her friends about God's love. Suddenly she had an idea. She could invite them to a birthday party. Everyone enjoys a party! After the party she told her friends how she became a Christian. Soon other Christians were copying her idea.

Education, money and a pension don't fill the empty place in people's lives when they ignore God. Thousands have turned to witchcraft and spiritism, and thousands more are turning to New Age teaching, to Jehovah's Witnesses and the Mormons, to try to fill that place.

They do not know that the empty place in their lives can truly be filled only by Jesus.

## DO YOU KNOW?

Uruguay is the smallest country in South America, but has one of the highest standards of living in the whole continent.

## You Can Pray for Uruguay

### Dear Lord Jesus

1 Help Christians to find exciting new ways to share their faith.

2 Call many Christians with the gift of teaching to train young people in your ways.

3 When people become dissatisfied with the emptiness of their lives, may they meet Christians who can show them that you are 'the way, the truth and the life'.

4 May evangelistic teams from Brazil and Argentina know the power of your Holy Spirit as they tell Uruguayans that you want them to follow you.

5 Show Uruguayans who are following spiritism and witchcraft that these come from the devil.

6 Use Christian books and leaflets to help people understand that only you can give them real joy and peace.

7 May every Christian radio programme bring people to new life in you.

## The book van

'How can we tell our school friends about Jesus?' Maria asked her father, the pastor of a small country church in Uruguay. 'You know it's against the law to talk about religion in school or university.'

'I have an idea,' her father replied. 'Carlos will be here any day now with the C.L.C.* book van. I'm sure he'll be able to help us.'

Every two months Carlos visited churches and little groups of Christians scattered throughout Uruguay. They looked forward to his coming and were eager to buy Christian books from him.

When Carlos heard about Maria's problem he had a suggestion. 'Here are some pens and pencils,' he said. 'See, they all have Bible texts on them. Take them to school and sell them to your friends. We'll pray that God's Word will speak to them and their families, and that outside school they

will want to talk to you about God. There's no law against that!'

*Christian Literature Crusade

# VIETNAM

## WHERE BRAVE PEOPLE FOLLOW JESUS

### Not afraid!

One by one, as secretly as possible, the *montagnard* Christians climbed the notched pole into Nai's bamboo-and-thatch house for the prayer meeting. They knew they would be punished if the agents of the communist government caught them, but they were not afraid.

Suddenly two men burst into the house and grabbed Nai. 'You're under arrest,' they shouted. 'There is no God!' They marched Nai away in the darkness. Like shadows, the other Christians slipped away home, wondering who had betrayed them.

Nai was sentenced to reap a large field of rice by himself, using only a small sickle. The pastor called the Christians together and soon a hundred people arrived to help Nai cut and thresh the rice. The communist agents were furious. They arrested the pastor and put him in prison. 'We'll put a stop to Christianity!' they declared. They couldn't!

Throughout the mountain region of Vietnam thousands of tribal people, or *montagnards*, are becoming Christians. The communists have burned their homes and put many, even children, in prison. Some they have tortured and killed, but they have not been able to make the Christians stop telling others about Jesus.

The Vietnamese are quite different from the *montagnards*, and live in villages, towns and cities on the coastal plain. They, too, are coming to know Jesus as their Saviour, and many of them know what it is to suffer because they are Christians. When pastors have been put in prison, they have gone on sharing the Good News about Jesus with all the other prisoners and with their guards as well!

## DO YOU KNOW?

Vietnam is a long, narrow country in South East Asia. On the map it looks like a carrying-pole with a basket of rice hung from each end. The two areas which look like baskets are the most fertile parts of the whole country.

## Good News

Before the French came to Vietnam, Roman Catholic missionaries had started to teach the Vietnamese. In 1911 missionaries from the Christian and Missionary Alliance began preaching the Good News about Jesus. Soon there were Vietnamese and tribal Christians in towns and villages throughout the land. Their churches are still called the 'Good News' Churches.

Although many Christians have suffered for their faith under communism, the church has grown and goes on growing. Some meet in church buildings and others in homes. Outspoken pastors and Christians are still put in prison, but they know that God is with them always.

## Changes

From 1975 until February 1994 the United States of America would not trade with Vietnam because of the harsh and unfair way in which the government was treating some people.

Since then, Christian aid organizations and businessmen have gone to Vietnam to show the people that they are not forgotten. It is often difficult for them to get permission to help those who most need it.

In 1994 the Christians were overjoyed when the Vietnamese government at last allowed Bibles to be printed again, and for a Bible school to be opened in Da Nang. Once again a few Christians are being trained to be pastors and evangelists.

The Vietnamese Christians have shown us how strong their faith is. They have not let hardship, persecution or imprisonment stop them from following Jesus or telling others about him. When I pray for them I am reminded of some words in Psalm 56:11: 'In God I will trust; I will not be afraid. What can man do to me?'

## War!

France ruled Vietnam from 1858 to 1954. During that time some Vietnamese people became very rich and lived in magnificent houses in the cities. The peasants and fishermen, however, were poor. Even now the peasants' homes are made of woven bamboo and thatch. Fishermen and their families often live all their lives on small boats.

In 1954 the Vietnamese defeated the French in a fierce battle but that did not bring peace. Vietnam was divided into two parts: the North which was under communist rule, and the 'free' South.

The communists wanted to control the South as well, and sent guerrilla soldiers to force the people to follow them. America started to help the South, and the North fought back. Many people died in this terrible war which the communists won in 1975.

Foreigners, including missionaries, fled the country. Thousands of South Vietnamese who were afraid the communists would treat them badly, tried to escape in small boats. Often these boats were old and in bad repair. Sometimes there were too many people in them and they sank in tropical storms. Others were attacked by pirates. Some did reach safety. You may even have a family of Vietnamese 'boat-people' living near you.

## You Can Pray for Vietnam

### Dear Lord Jesus

1 When life is hard and difficult for the Christians in Vietnam, please help them to keep on following you.

2 Help all the pastors and Christians to be brave as they tell others about you, even when they are in prison.

3 May there soon be real peace in Vietnam, and freedom for everyone to worship you openly.

4 Please send Christians to care for lonely, hurt and unhappy children whose parents have died.

5 Thank you that the government has given permission for Bibles to be printed in Vietnam. May each Christian family soon have one of their own.

6 Help the students at the new Bible School to become faithful pastors and evangelists.

7 May there soon be a government in Vietnam which will be fair to all the people who live there, and honest towards other countries.

# MISSIONARY KIDS

## BELONGING TO TWO WORLDS

'David, what's it like in England?' Paul asked. 'I was only four when my family were there last. I've forgotten what it's like, and I feel scared about lots of things. Were you scared?'

### Special

David remembered how bewildered he'd felt when they'd arrived at Heathrow Airport in London. Everything had seemed so enormous, exciting and a bit frightening, and there were so many people rushing around. He'd made sure he'd kept close to Dad! He'd liked the moving walkways and escalators, but he'd wondered how they would ever find their own cases on the carousels packed with luggage.

'Yes, I was scared of lots of things, even though I knew I'd be seeing my grandparents and all the rest of our family,' David replied. 'I wondered how I'd get on with them, but granny and grandad made me feel very special. We had lots of treats, like hamburgers at McDonald's, and going to the pantomime in the local theatre. I'd never seen anything like that theatre before!'

### Changes

Paul and David are both nine years old, and are students at a small, international boarding school for MKs (missionaries' children) in West Africa. David and his family have recently returned from a year in England, and Paul and his family will soon be going on home leave.

Paul grinned. 'I'm looking forward to things like that, and to television. Dad's even promised to take me to see a Premier Division football match.

'I know there'll be lots of big shops and plenty of things to buy,' Paul continued. 'But how will I know what to choose? And what about the food in England? Did you like it? Is it very different from the food we have here?'

David laughed and said, 'Well, I missed peanut stew! But there were lots of other nice things to eat. We could have sausages every day in England if we wanted to, but they're such a treat here.'

### Two schools

'How did you get on when you went to school?' Paul asked. 'Our school here is so small and all the teachers are our friends. We know everyone, and we're like a big family, and it's fun being here. We do so many things together. What's it like going to school in England?'

'At first my new school seemed so huge,' David replied. 'There were almost as many kids in my class as we have in the whole school here. I wondered whether I'd make friends, and if the other kids would think me strange because I didn't know much about life in England. I wondered whether my school work would be good enough. It was! I was even top of the class sometimes. And it was great having enough kids for a football team!

'Sometimes I got fed up with having to tell the class about life in Africa, but I knew a lot more about Africa than they did! They really liked hearing about the monkeys, elephants and crocodiles we see here. They couldn't believe that we'd even kept a gazelle as a pet.

'I told them about living in the village with my parents and the fun I'd had with the African children when I was little, before I came to boarding school. They seemed really sad when I told them how lonely I am sometimes when I go home to the village during school holidays. I told them that I still played with my African friends, but it's not the same. My life is so different from theirs because they never leave their village except to go to their fields or to the market.

'Actually, my class back in England liked hearing about our school here! I told them about our fun times, and about our games and sports and some of the tricks we play on each other in the dorm. They enjoyed hearing about our visits to the cotton fields and local markets. I told them about some of the difficult things as well, such as the heat and insects, and only having electricity for a few hours every day, and how ill I felt when I had malaria.

'Some of them couldn't believe that we studied the Bible every day and had our own church service on Sundays, and that we really enjoyed it. A few of my class in England went to Sunday school, but most of them didn't.'

## More than one culture

As missionaries' children, like Paul and David, grow up they have many unusual experiences. Sometimes they travel a great deal and live in fascinating places. They meet lots of people and enjoy having friends from all round the world. On the other hand, they sometimes feel very lonely, especially when they have to say 'Goodbye' to their friends or move to a new place.

Sometimes being part of more than one culture as they grow up can be very hard for them. They do not feel they belong to the country where they are growing up, and they don't always feel completely at home in the country their parents call 'home'. But it is a life full of interesting experiences, and because of what they go through they are often good at understanding other people and their needs.

Will you pray that God will help them to feel at home wherever they live? And if ever an MK comes to your school, will you be a special friend to him or her?

# ACEHNESE

## PROUD MUSLIMS OF SUMATRA

### A forbidden book

'What's that book you're reading? Here, let me see it.' Ahmat tried to hide the book, but his friend snatched it away. 'Why, it's a Christian book. Where did you get it from? You know you will be punished for having it, if you're caught, and the book will be burned. We Acehnese are Muslims, and every day we declare our faith when we repeat, "There is no God but Allah." Christians claim they worship one God, but they also say they worship God the Father, God the Son and Mary.'

'Give it back to me,' Ahmat pleaded. 'It's part of the *Injil* (the Gospel) and tells the story of Jesus. He was so kind and good, and helped many people. He made sick people well, and brought dead people back to life. They are wonderful stories, and Jesus must have been a very special person. I can't see anything wrong with reading a book like that. After all, it says in the Koran that we should read all the holy books, even the *Injil*. I wish someone could tell me more about Jesus.'

'Take it, but don't let anyone else see it.' His friend thrust the book into Ahmat's hand. 'Remember what I've told you.' Ahmat was glad to have the book back again. It belonged to his brother.

Like many Acehnese men, Ahmat's brother had gone away from home to work. The women are left behind to look after the rice and pepper fields, while the men earn money. Ahmat's brother went to Jakarta, the capital of Indonesia. He often felt lonely there until one evening in a restaurant he met some friendly Indonesian Christians. They told him about God who loves him and wants to be his friend. They gave him this book about Jesus.

### Muslim traders

The Acehnese (pronounced *Ah-chey-nees*) live in the province of Aceh at the northernmost tip of Sumatra. As long ago as the 13th century traders from the Middle East travelled to Sumatra bringing with them goods to trade for silk and pepper. More importantly, these traders brought with them their own Muslim faith.

As the years passed by, the Acehnese adopted Islam as their own religion. They think of Aceh as the 'verandah of Mecca'. One of the duties a good Muslim is expected to do, at least once in his lifetime, is to go on the Hajj. This is the pilgrimage to Mecca, the most holy city of Islam, in Saudi Arabia. Devout Acehnese Muslims used to make the long journey by sea, but now they are more likely to go by plane.

Most people in Indonesia are Muslims, but the Acehnese feel that many of them have let other things creep into their lives and weaken their faith. The Acehnese are very proud of being Muslims and have their own Muslim schools and universities.

## You Can Pray for the Acehnese

### Dear Lord Jesus

1 Help Christians from other countries who live and work in Aceh to be both wise and bold in their witness for you.

2 May Acehnese people who travel to other places meet friendly Christians who will be kind to them and show them how much you care for them.

3 Use each copy of the Injil and New Testament to bring an Acehnese person to know you.

4 Help the few Acehnese Christians to be true to you always, even if they are badly treated because of their faith.

5 Break the power of Islam in the lives of the proud Acehnese people.

6 Help the people who are preparing Christian radio programmes to make them so interesting that many Acehnese will want to listen to them.

7 May your Holy Spirit show the Acehnese that, although Islam demands obedience to its laws, it cannot give them the power to keep them.

# Keep out!

The Acehnese fought against the Portuguese, the English and the Dutch who invaded their land. They did not want to be ruled by them, nor did they want the Christian religion of these countries. They wanted to be free.

Although Christian missionaries have been able to work in other parts of Indonesia, the Acehnese have never allowed them to preach the gospel in their land. Only a few Acehnese have ever become Christians, and they live abroad or in other parts of Indonesia.

There are some Christians living in Aceh, but they have come from other countries and from different parts of Indonesia. They have built churches there, but the Acehnese are not happy about this. Sometimes they have burned down the churches, because they do not want any of their own people to become Christians. Now you will understand why Ahmat had to hide his copy of the Injil.

Does this mean that we should forget all about the Acehnese? Shall we forget that God wants men and women everywhere to follow him? That includes the people of Aceh. God has promised that there will be Acehnese in heaven, but how will they hear the gospel? Your prayers and mine will make the difference!

# BALINESE

## WHOSE HOME IS THE ISLAND OF THE GODS

### Beautiful island

Bali is a beautiful island in the long necklace of Indonesian islands you can see on the map. It has high mountains and volcanoes, sandy beaches, dazzling flowers, brilliant rice fields of green and gold and thousands of ornate temples. More than a million tourists visit Bali every year, and it's no wonder they often call it 'the island of the gods' or even 'the last paradise'.

### Beautiful people

The Balinese people, too, are very beautiful, with smiling, gentle faces. Tourists love to watch them perform their graceful *legong* dances, which tell stories of gods and demons, witches and kidnapped princesses. The dancers are young girls dressed in cloth of gold and scarlet, green and blue. On their shiny black hair they wear elaborate head-dresses of glittering gold decorated with bright, tropical flowers.

It's not surprising that there are thousands of temples on Bali, because the Balinese are Hindus and worship many gods. Long before they became Hindus the Balinese already had many gods. They worship these, too. They believe it is very important to keep on the right side of them all.

### Invitation to the gods

At the beginning of every year (the year in Bali is only 210 days long), the Balinese hold a special feast for the gods. At this feast they bring their gods, made of wood, stone and coins, out from their shrines. For ten days the people invite the gods to join them in feasting and dancing. At the end of that time the gods are put away again.

### Spirits of the ancestors

The Balinese believe that the spirits of their gods and ancestors live in the mountains. When they build their homes, they make sure that the room with the spirit-altar faces the mountains.

They believe that what happens to them when they die is very important. Sometimes it takes a family several years to save enough money for an ornate funeral tower to be built, and for the cremation ceremony to take place. Only then can the soul of the dead person take its place with the spirits of all the other ancestors in the mountains.

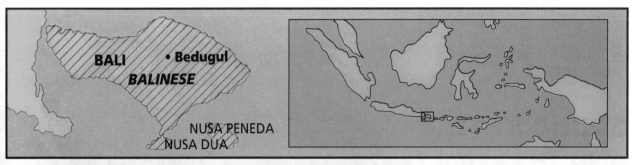

BALI • Bedugul
BALINESE

NUSA PENEDA
NUSA DUA

## Jesus' power

At present there are not many Balinese Christians. Sometimes their Hindu neighbours treat them badly because they are afraid that their gods will be angry if people follow Jesus.

Eight-year-old Nyoman was afraid because other people in the village had done unkind things to his family because they are Christians. 'Why won't the people in the village let us have water for our fields? They never help us as they help each other. What have we done?' he asked. 'The other children make fun of me and won't play with me. They even say that one night, when I'm asleep, the gods will come and punish me because I don't follow them.'

'Don't be afraid, Nyoman,' his father replied. 'We must trust Jesus to help us. He has promised that he will always be with us and that nothing has any power to take his love away.

'People in the village think the gods are angry because we have become Christians. They are doing these things because they want us to turn back to our old gods. But we know that Jesus has set us free from their power and will look after us even when we are asleep. Let's talk to him about it and ask him to take away your fears.'

Although Christians are often treated badly by their Hindu neighbours, they want them to know that Jesus loves them. They try to show them this by helping them in practical ways. They want them to know, too, that Christianity isn't a dull religion which belongs to the white people, so Christians are beginning to tell Bible stories the Balinese way, in dance and mime.

One by one Balinese are coming to know Jesus as the friend who is with them always. These people want many more Balinese to discover that Jesus is far greater and more powerful than all the thousands of gods they keep in their shrines and bring out on special occasions.

## DO YOU KNOW?

A Balinese legend says the island was once flat and nothing grew there. When the neighbouring island of Java became Muslim, the Hindu gods moved to Bali, where they made mountains where they could live. Water from the mountains made the island fertile.

## You Can Pray for the Balinese

### Dear Lord Jesus

1 Please help Christians to find practical ways of showing your love to their Hindu friends and neighbours.

2 Give courage and power to Balinese Christians to witness for you in their villages.

3 Help Balinese people to understand that you are almighty and are more powerful than all the gods and goddesses they worship.

4 Help Christians to know that the evil spirits have no power to harm them when they trust in you.

5 May whole families come to have faith in you, so that children can learn to trust you and follow you when they are young.

6 May your Holy Spirit help groups who use Balinese-style dance and mime to tell the Christian story clearly.

7 Thank you for the Bible in Balinese. Help Christians to read your Word and follow what they learn.

# BEJA

## BOUND BY FEAR AND THE EVIL EYE

### A boy is born

Halimeh held her baby son in her arms. It was hot and dark in the tiny house, with its roof and walls of woven matting. 'Only one more day,' she thought, 'and I can go out.' She could hear Abdul, her husband, putting a bundle of sticks on the fire burning outside the house.

Ever since his son had been born, Abdul had kept the fire alight day and night to frighten away evil spirits in case they harmed his wife and son. 'Tomorrow,' he said to himself, 'I shall see my son. He will be 40 days old and, after the custom of our people, I shall see him for the first time. Praise be to Allah that my wife has given me a son.'

Abdul smiled. In his mind he could still hear the trills and chants of congratulation when his son was born. How different it would have been if the baby had been a girl. No-one would have congratulated him then.

'Tomorrow will be a special day,' he thought. 'We'll kill a sheep and the elders will give my son the name they have chosen for him. He will become a Muslim, like all the Beja people. Now, though, I'd better go and milk my goats.'

### Always hungry

Abdul sang as he milked his goats, praising his animals. As usual there wasn't much milk. His family would be hungry. They were hungry every day. Abdul sighed. 'If only it would

rain, I could sow a little seed in the wadi (dried-up river-bed) and then perhaps we should have some grain. As it is, I'll have to sell another goat. If only it would rain, the grass would grow, and there would be leaves on the thorn bushes. The animals would have food to eat then and they would give more milk.

'What can I do? I really don't want to go and live in Port Sudan and work for money, like so many Beja have done. I want to be free to follow the ways of my people and live here as we have always done.'

### Unconquered

Most of the million and a half Beja live in north-east Sudan. For more than 4,000 years the

Beja people have roamed this hot, dry desert land and the bleak Red Sea Hills in their search for pasture for their herds of camels, cattle, sheep and goats. It is a harsh place in which to live. The Beja keep to themselves and don't make friends easily with strangers.

In the distant past Egyptians, Greeks and Romans all tried to conquer them, but without success. Last century the Beja became famous for a short time when they won a battle against a well-equipped part of the British Army. The only weapons the Beja had were spears and sticks. Soon the 'Fuzzy-Wuzzies', as they were affectionately known because of their frizzy hair, were forgotten.

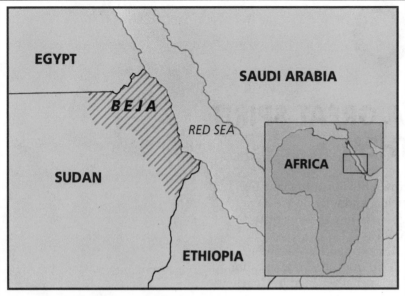

EGYPT

BEJA

SUDAN

SAUDI ARABIA

RED SEA

AFRICA

ETHIOPIA

# Fear of the evil eye

The Beja have been Muslims for about 800 years. Very few of them really understand the Muslim faith, or pray and fast as Muslim law demands. Instead, most of them follow their old beliefs and customs. They are afraid of the evil eye and jinns (evil spirits), which, they believe, want to harm them and make them ill. They are bound by fear, superstition and hunger. Life is very hard for the Beja.

Only a few Beja people have ever become Christians. In 1978, for the first time, some Christian missionaries were given permission to start medical work among them. Do you think the Beja were grateful? No! Very soon the local Beja leaders forced the missionaries to leave. The missionary team began their work again, in another area. Once again they were forced to leave.

Jesus died for the Beja as well as for you and me. He promises the Beja freedom from superstition, fear and the evil spirits which hold them so tightly in their grip. Will the Beja ever listen to the message God wants them to hear? Will they ever hold out their hands to God?

## You Can Pray for the Beja

### Dear Lord Jesus

1 Please bring help to the Beja, who are often hungry because of drought and famine.

2 May Christian workers find ways to help the Beja and show them that you love them and have not forgotten them.

3 Help the Beja people to listen to those who tell them about your love and want to help them.

4 May those Beja who understand Arabic and have radios listen to Christian radio programmes in Arabic.

5 May there soon be Christian radio programmes in To-Bedawie that every Beja can understand.

6 Send people to study the To-Bedawie language. Help them to put it into writing and then translate your Word for the Beja people.

7 Help the Beja to want to learn to read.

# BIJAGO

## WHO BELIEVE IN A GREAT SPIRIT WHO PUNISHES THEM

### Making the fields

Carlos is a puzzled little Bijago boy. 'Why do we have to move to the island of Rubane every rainy season?' he demanded. 'Why can't we live here all the time? Why do we have to sacrifice an animal before we cut down the forest to make our fields, and why do we have to go there to plant our rice anyway?'

Carlos stood by his father asking question after question. Dad had sharpened his machete (a large knife) and now he was busy catching the chickens and

## Thatched houses, thatched temples

The beautiful Bijagos Islands, with their white, sandy beaches, palm trees and brightly-coloured birds, belong to Guinea-Bissau, and the people who live there are called Bijago. Although the islands are so lovely, the people who live there are very poor. Many live in round houses made of mud, with thatched roofs. The houses are dark inside and the villages are sometimes very dirty. The people are often ill, their crops are poor and their cattle very weak.

The Bijago are animists. They believe in a Great Spirit who made them but will not help them. Instead they think that this Great Spirit sends them punishment and disaster. They build elaborate temples of mud and thatch. In the middle of each temple is an altar surrounded by fetishes (things which are worshipped) and carved idols. The Bijago are afraid of the *iran* (evil spirits) and hope that by sacrificing animals and performing special ceremonies they will be kept safe from harm.

putting them into a woven palm-branch basket. Carlos glanced across at his mother. She was collecting together all the pots and pans, the kerosene lamp, her grass skirts and everything else the family would need for the next six months. Everyone in the village was busy with their belongings and babies, pigs and chickens.

'It's our custom,' his father replied. 'Rubane is a sacred place belonging to our village. The *iran* will not let us build our homes there, and they will send danger and sickness on our village if anyone dies there. That is why the witchdoctor sacrifices an animal even before we start to cut down the forest. Don't you remember that he gave us a piece of the meat to cook in the part of the forest where we made our fields last year? We call that "paying the ground". Only by doing that can we hope that the *iran* will not harm us.'

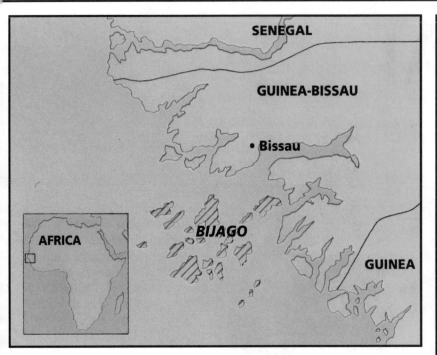

SENEGAL

GUINEA-BISSAU

• Bissau

AFRICA

BIJAGO

GUINEA

## DO YOU KNOW?

A Bijago woman chooses her husband and proposes to him with an offering of food. She builds a house and then invites the man she has chosen to live with her there.

What a noise there was at the port! People scrambled to find places for themselves and their belongings in the small dug-out canoes which they would paddle across to Rubane Island. Soon the village was deserted. They would not return for another six months.

### Changed by Jesus!

Forty years ago the village of Ancarave, on the island of Uno, was just like any other Bijago village. People were sick and afraid, and their animals weak. This wasn't surprising, because they got their water for drinking, cooking and washing from a dirty, slimy pool.

The witchdoctors made offerings to the *iran*, but nothing improved. One day some Christian visitors came to the island. 'You do not have to be afraid of the *iran*,' they told the people. 'The priests and witch-doctors make sacrifices, but you still get ill and don't have enough to eat. Your children and animals die. God is far more powerful than any of the *iran*. He loves you so much that he sent his only Son, Jesus, as a sacrifice for you. If you trust in him, he will help you.' Some of

the people became Christians, and the visitors taught them to follow Jesus. The village chief went on following the *iran* because he was afraid.

These Christians wanted to help the Bijago people in other ways, too. They translated the Bible into the Bijago language, and in 1973 Tear Fund helped them to dig a well in the village of Ancarave. What a difference clean, fresh water made to them! This helped their village chief to see that God loves the Bijago people and wants to help them. He became a Christian and burned all his idols. The Bijago Christians were so happy, they danced and sang for joy. When other villages saw what Jesus had done for the people of Ancarave, some wanted to follow him, too.

Now there are Christians on several of the islands. They are glad God helps them when life is difficult, but some have forgotten how hard life was when they lived in fear of the *iran*. They still need missionar-ies, evangelists and pastors who can teach them more about Jesus and God's love.

## You can pray for the Bijago

### Dear Lord Jesus

1 Please help Papa, a Bijago pastor, to be a faithful teacher and example to the people of the islands.

2 Give Christians the courage to take the Good News to all the islands.

3 Help new believers to know the power of your Holy Spirit so that they will be strong in you.

4 May many Bijago people see you in the lives of Christians, and want to follow you.

5 Bijago people have no need to read, so most cannot do so. Help Christians to want to read your Word, which will show them how they should live.

6 May more young Bijago Christians go to Bible School and learn how to teach others to follow you.

7 Help Christians to know that your power is greater than the power of the *iran*.

# BURYAT

## BUDDHISTS IN SIBERIA

### A special visitor

'Look, look! There he is! There's the Dalai Lama!' Temudjin was so thrilled he could scarcely stand still. 'It's so exciting that he has come to our Buryat Republic and that we should see him!'

'Who would have thought the Russian Government would give him permission to visit us?' his uncle said. 'I've heard the Chinese are not at all pleased that he has been allowed to come. But why shouldn't he come? After all, we Buryat are Buddhists, and the Centre for Buddhism for the whole of Russia is right here in Ulan Ude.'

Gaily-coloured prayer flags fluttered over the monastery. In his hand Temudjin held his prayer beads and let them slip, one by one, through his fingers. Earlier in the day he and his uncle had gone to the temple and had set the prayer wheels spinning.

It was 1991. Thousands of people had gathered outside the monastery school in Ulan Ude for its first anniversary. The rhythmic sound of temple gongs and the chanting of monks throbbed out over the crowd, then all was quiet. The Dalai Lama started to speak, urging the people to put the years of communism behind them and return to their Buddhist beliefs.

### Home in Siberia

Most Buryats live in southern Siberia in the beautiful valleys and mountains around Lake Baikal, but some live in Mongolia and China. For hundreds of years Buryats have bred horses and reared cattle. At one time the Buryats were animists, but several centuries ago Buryats who lived to the east of Lake Baikal became Buddhists. They kept many of their old animistic beliefs and so the two religions mingled together.

Buryat boys went to the Buddhist monasteries for their schooling and often became monks. At the beginning of the twentieth century one man in every five became a monk. All this changed after the Russian Revolution, and by the end of the 1930s not one monastery remained open.

### Why help the Buryat?

In 1817 three English missionaries travelled to Siberia. They had permission from the Tsar of Russia himself. He even gave them land and money to help them in their work among the Buryats.

'Why ever do you want to help the Buryats?' Russians living in the region wanted to know. 'We certainly don't think much of them!' The Buryats, too, wondered why the missionaries had come.

While they were there those missionaries translated the whole of the Bible into the Buryat language. Unfortunately, the Buryat script has been changed several times since then, and now no one can read that translation.

A few Buryats became Christians, and then in 1841 the Tsar sent word to the missionaries that they must leave. The Russian Orthodox Church set up its own mission to the Buryat and built churches. Still the Buryat did not become Christians.

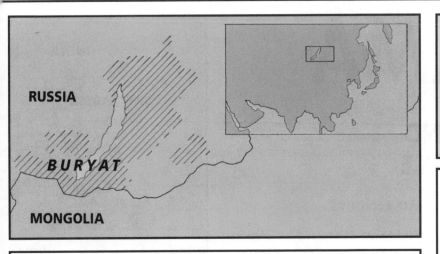

### DO YOU KNOW?

The Buryat Republic is more than twice the size of England, but there are more than eight times as many people living in London than in the whole of the Republic.

## You Can Pray for the Buryat

**Dear Lord Jesus**

1 Please show the Buryat that, however hard they try, they cannot make their next life better than this one.

2 Show the Buryat that the Dalai Lama is not a god. He is only a man.

3 Help Christians to make friends with Buryats, and to tell them that you love them and came to take away their sin.

4 May the caring lives of Christians who live in the Buryat region speak to the hearts of the Buryat people.

5 Help those who are making a new translation of the Bible. May it be in words that everyone can understand.

6 Thank you that the Buryat can choose which religion they want to follow. May many choose to follow you.

7 May the Buryat come to know that you alone are God, and that you want to be a special friend to each one of them.

# More special visitors

Temudjin lives in Ulan Ude, the capital of the Buryat Republic. He enjoys going to the state school with his friends. All of them had gone to the first anniversary of the new monastery school and were excited because they had heard the Dalai Lama speak.

'He spoke words of wisdom,' one of Temudjin's friends said. 'We must learn to follow the ways of the Buddha. It's not easy when we've been taught atheism by the communists and told that we must get rid of all religion.'

'What about those foreign teachers who've come to our school?' asked another. 'They tell us about Christianity and about Jesus. They say that he paid for our sins by dying for us. How can anyone do that? Even the Dalai Lama can't. Buddhism tells us that only we ourselves can pay the price for our own sins. We go on paying for them each time we're reborn.'

'My uncle says our rosary beads and prayer wheels are to help us meditate,' Temudjin said, 'but I like what the Christian teachers told us about prayer. They said that their God is Almighty and is everywhere. He always listens to his people when they pray and talk with him. They even said their God sent his only Son to take the punishment for our sins. I think I would like to know more about him.'

What is the future for these young Buryats? Who will they follow? Your prayers can help them to decide.

# CHAKMA

## AN ANCIENT AND TROUBLED PEOPLE

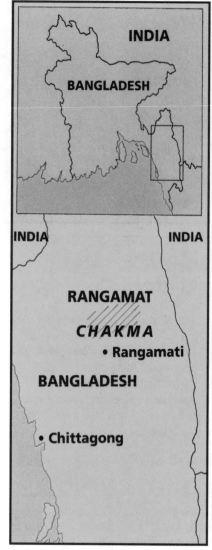

### Through the maze

Debapriya Roy tried to open his eyes. As he did so, the room seemed to go round and round in circles. For a little while he thought he was a child again, taking part in the *Bohu Chakra* ceremonies in his home village. With all the other village children he was trying to find his way through the complicated maze in front of the temple to the statue of Buddha.

'If I'm first, and don't touch anything on the way,' he thought, 'then everyone will say I am righteous and good. I do want to be first to reach the statue!'

### An accident

Suddenly Debapriya realized he wasn't a child, but had been dreaming. He was in hospital and his legs felt heavy and useless. He heard the doctor say to his mother, 'He'll be all right.' He remembered then that he'd been in an accident and had been thrown from his motorbike.

Debapriya wanted to get better as quickly as possible. After all, he was only nineteen years old. He was the oldest son in his family, and his family were important people. He was the

cousin of the Chakma king.

But Debapriya did not get better, and his parents decided to take him to the Memorial Christian Hospital at Malumghat. 'There's a very special doctor there called Dr Olsen,' a friend told them. Before Dr Olsen operated on him, he prayed in the name of Jesus. Debapriya had never heard anyone pray like that before.

He still did not get better. He felt very sad and miserable. He was sure he would never walk again. He would not be able to continue working as an engineer. Sometimes Debapriya wondered what he would do, because he was sure he would be a cripple.

# Buddhists

The Chakma people are Buddhists living in Bangladesh, where most people are Muslims. The Chakma, and other tribal groups, have lived in the central part of the Chittagong Hill Tracts of southeast Bangladesh for more than two and a half thousand years. Many of them are farmers. This is their homeland.

Bangladesh is an over-crowded country. In recent years many Bengali people have tried to settle in the less crowded Chittagong Hill Tracts. This has caused a lot of fighting between the tribal people and the Bengalis, and many have died. Now few people are allowed to visit this part of Bangladesh.

God has his plan for the Chakma people and is putting that plan into action. Men like Debapriya are part of that plan as they show their people that true peace and hope are found only as they trust in God.

## A new life

The doctors and nurses were very kind to him. They often sat by his bed and talked and prayed with him. One day Debapriya started to read the Bible they had left by the side of his bed. As he read the stories about Jesus he began to feel at peace.

'I want to become a Christian,' he told Dr Olsen. There, in his hospital room, Debapriya gave his life to the Lord Jesus. He was one of the first Chakma ever to become a Christian.

## Help for my people

Gradually Debapriya began to get better. Soon he was able to get about in his wheel chair and then managed to walk for short distances. 'I want to go home and help my people,' he decided. 'They must all hear the good news of eternal life in Jesus Christ.'

When the doctor heard what Debapriya wanted to do he said, 'Many of your people are well educated. The best way you can help them is to translate the Bible into the Chakma language.'

When Debapriya left hospital he did two things. He studied how to translate the Bible, and he trained to become a medical technician so that he could earn his living and help people who were ill. You can be sure he told the people who came to him that they did not have to struggle through a maze of sin and darkness to find the way of peace. He told them that Jesus

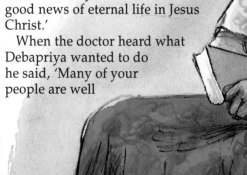

had come to show them the way to God and to give them peace.

When Debapriya started to translate the New Testament, there were very few Chakma Christians. Six years later, in 1991, when he completed the translation of the New Testament, there were about 80 Christians! Now he is translating the Old Testament.

## You Can Pray for the Chakma

### Dear Lord Jesus

1 Thank you for Debapriya Roy. Please help him and others as they translate the Old Testament into the Chakma language. May it be an accurate translation.

2 May many Chakma people want to read the New Testament and, as they read, may your Holy Spirit help them to understand it.

3 Show the Chakma people that only you can guide them through the maze of life and give them hope and peace.

4 May Chakma Christians be eager to share their faith with their friends and families.

5 May the children in Christian families learn to trust you to help them every day, especially to be good and to do right things.

6 May the government be fair to both the Chakma and the Bengali peoples.

7 Please bring peace to the Chittagong Hill Tracts, in the place of unrest and guerrilla warfare.

# DAI

## FROM THE LAND OF TWELVE THOUSAND RICE FIELDS

What fun the children are having! Laughing and shouting with glee, they are happily splashing everyone with water. No-one seems to mind in the least. After all, this is the Dai New Year, and the Water-Throwing Festival is only part of the fun.

In south-west China, on the borders of Myanmar and Laos, is a region called Xishuangbanna (pronounced *Shish-wang-banna*). This is the home of the Dai people. Monkeys, elephants, tigers, bears, deer and even peacocks live in the thick, lush forests which cover the high mountains. Beautiful flowers bloom in the forests, too.

The Dai people live in houses of wood, bamboo and thatch which are built on tall stilts. Pigs and hens make themselves at home under the houses. All round their houses the Dai grow coconut palms, banana, papaya and mango trees, pineapples and peppers. Then, of course, there are many paddy fields, for Xishuangbanna means the land of twelve thousand rice fields.

## Making merit

The Dai people are Buddhists, and in every village there is a temple. Seven-year-old Artuk tried to be brave as he waved goodbye to his parents and set out with his big brother, who was taking him to the monastery. Forty other little boys were already there. 'It's your turn to have your head shaved, Artuk,' said a monk. 'Here is a saffron-coloured robe for you. Wear it every day for the three years you are here.'

'Will you teach us to read?' Artuk asked respectfully. 'Yes, we start tomorrow,' replied the monk. 'You will learn to read the sacred Buddhist scriptures. You will earn merit for yourself and for your whole family, which will help you in your next life.'

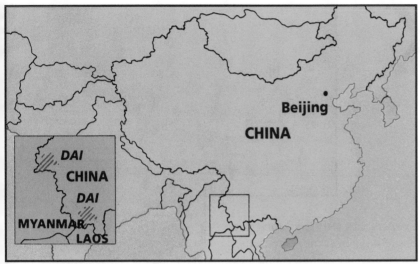

The Dai believe that water is the source of life on earth, and that it is also a sign of purity and beauty. Every village has a well. Each year, on the day it was completed, a special celebration is held, and the well is cleaned and its ornate covering is repainted.

## Good triumphs

The Dai people love to tell stories. 'Daddy, please tell us the story of the Water-Throwing Festival again,' the children asked after they had eaten their evening meal. Like many Dai stories, this one is about the victory of good over evil.

'Once upon a time,' their father began, 'our people were ruled by a powerful demon-king who made life very hard for them. He had seven wives, but the youngest, Yu Xiang, was a kind and gentle person. She did not like to see the people suffer. "I wish the demon-king would die," she thought, "so that the Dai people can be free from his evil power."

'The demon-king was very fond of Yu Xiang. One day he told her, "My power is in the single white hair on my head. I can be defeated only if it is pulled out and tied around my neck." That night, when he was fast asleep, Yu Xiang pulled out that one white hair and tied it tightly round his neck and beheaded him.

'Everyone was happy because the demon-king was dead, but as soon as his head touched the ground it burst into flames and burned everything it touched. At last brave Yu Xiang was able to pick up the head. When she did, the fire stopped. When she put it down, the fire started again. "Quick, quick," the people shouted, and rushed to throw water over Yu Xiang to put out the fire and wash away the blood. Now, when we keep the Water-Throwing Festival, we remember this story. We believe the water will make us pure and clean and keep us from harm.'

The Dai do not yet know that 'making merit', or throwing water at one another, can never make their hearts clean or make them fit for heaven. There are a few Dai Christians, but they do not have a Bible or any Christian books in their language. How are they going to learn that God sent his Son, Jesus, to defeat all the powers of darkness and evil, and to give pure, clean hearts to all who follow him? Who will tell them?

## You Can Pray for the Dai

### Dear Lord Jesus

1 Give courage to the few Dai Christians as they tell other Dai people about your love for them.

2 Show them that only you can set them free from the power of evil spirits.

3 Help them to understand that becoming monks and 'making merit' will never earn them salvation.

4 May your Holy Spirit show them that you died to make them pure and clean, and fit for heaven.

5 Even though missionaries are not allowed to enter China, please send Christians who can show the Dai how much you care for them.

6 The Dai people have great fun in remembering their old legends. May they find much greater joy and happiness in following you.

7 Send Christians from other countries who will be able to translate the Bible into the Dai language.

# DAYAK

## FROM A LAND OF JUNGLES AND RIVERS

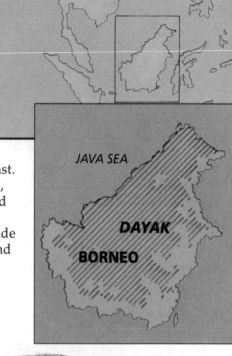

JAVA SEA

DAYAK

BORNEO

### The omen bird

'Stop!' Idjam called to the Dayak villagers following him along the trail through the jungle. 'I can hear the cry of the omen bird. See, there it is! Who knows what dangers it is warning us about? This is not a good day for us to plant our fields. Go back home! We'll have to try again tomorrow!'

'What have we done wrong?' Idjam wondered as he hurried back to the village. 'We offered a sacrifice to the spirits before we cut down the jungle to make our fields. We left some trees on the hill top, so that visiting spirits could have a place to rest. The trees and undergrowth all burnt well, and there was plenty of good ash, which means there should be a good harvest. Why are the spirits angry?'

The next day Idjam and the people from his village set out once again. This time they reached their fields on the steep mountainside without hearing the call of the omen bird. The men and boys made holes in the ground between the burnt-out tree stumps, using sharp-pointed sticks. The women and girls dropped a few rice seeds from their baskets into each hole. When harvest-time comes, they will cut the rice, stem by stem, with a knife.

Most Dayak live along the river banks and in the jungle areas of Kalimantan, in central Borneo. Once they were head-hunters, but that is all long past. Some have become Christians, but many are still animists and live in constant fear of evil spirits, which, they believe, hide in rocks, trees, rivers, caves and on the mountains, waiting to harm them or make them ill.

# Set free!

Hanji is the teacher in a village school. 'I remember the first time a missionary came to my village,' he said. 'I was a small boy, and frightened because I had never seen a white person before. He came in a boat like ours and stayed in our longhouse.

'Night after night he told us about Jesus, God's Son. He told us that Jesus had power over all the evil spirits, and could free us from our fears. I was often afraid of those spirits, especially when the witch doctor was around. I wanted that freedom more than anything, so I decided to follow Jesus, and so did some of my friends. At first the older men were afraid the spirits would be angry, because we had to burn all our charms, but when nothing bad happened to us, some of them also became Christians.

'The missionaries taught us boys to read. We were excited because we could read stories about Jesus. Later, some of us went to Bible School and learnt to become evangelists to our own Dayak people. Now I am the teacher in this village.'

Hanji glanced around. 'Look at the boys playing down at the river,' he complained. 'They should all be in school, but no one makes them go. It's the same in every village. Often their parents want them to stay at home and help feed the chickens and pigs, to go looking for food, or mind the little ones.

'Sometimes the children themselves decide they just don't want to come to school. That's sad. The Dayak way of life is changing, and it's important that they should be able to read and write. Of course, some children come every day because they want to go to high school in the town and perhaps to university later on.

'Nearly half the people in this village say they are Christians, but some of them think they don't need to come to church. How will they ever learn more about Jesus? The girls all come to Sunday School, and we have a happy time singing and learning Bible stories, but the boys – well, they prefer to play or go fishing. Those boys need to know Jesus if they are to be good husbands for our Christian girls!'

## DO YOU KNOW?

Dayak children are never punished with a smack. They may be laughed at, or made fun of instead, or told something terrible will happen to them. Often they are told lies to keep them happy.

## You Can Pray for the Dayak

### Dear Lord Jesus

1 Please show the Dayak that you are more powerful than all the evil spirits they believe are everywhere. Help them to know that they can trust you, even when they are afraid.

2 Help Dayak Christians to understand that you want them to know you as their special friend, and that they should spend time worshipping you and learning about you.

3 May the leaders of the village churches know the power of your Holy Spirit in their lives so that they will be able to lead others to know you and help them to live in a way that will please you.

4 May Dayak Christians be so eager to understand your Word that they will want to learn to read so they can study it themselves.

5 Be with Christian young people who go away from their villages to study in the towns. Help them always to be faithful to you.

6 Please may every church have a Sunday School with good teachers, so that the children can learn about you.

7 Bring many young men to know you and to follow you, so that they will be good Christian husbands for the lovely Christian girls.

# DRUZE

## FOLLOWERS OF A SECRET RELIGION

Do you find it hard to keep secrets? The Druze have an important secret they've kept for almost a thousand years!

The Druze live in the mountain regions of Lebanon, Syria, Israel and Jordan. Most of them are farmers who have olive groves and cherry and apple orchards on the hillsides, and grow vegetables in their carefully tended gardens. There is work for everyone, but still plenty of time to visit with friends and family. Some Druze live in the towns, but wherever they are, and whatever they do, they are known as hardworking people who can be trusted.

### The big secret

Their big secret is their religion. They are convinced that what they believe must be kept to themselves and never shared with outsiders. Of course many people have tried to find out what they do believe, but the Druze often mislead them. Their religion has to be kept a secret.

No one can ever become a Druze, he must be born one. A Druze believes that when he dies, his soul immediately enters a newborn Druze baby. That is the only way a person can become a Druze. When a Druze marries, he must only marry a

Druze. If he marries someone of another faith, he can no longer be a Druze.

Even among themselves, there are only a few people who know all the secrets about their religion. These are called 'Uqqal, the 'Informed' or 'Knowledge-able Ones'. Both men and women can become 'Uqqal, but they must be at least forty years old, and have spent long periods of time thinking about the secrets of their religion. They are the only ones who are allowed to study the 'Book of Wisdom', the Druze scriptures.

On Thursday evenings everyone in a Druze village meets in the *Khilwa*, or meeting-place. Samir and Salim watched as their parents joined the other villagers. Like most Druze, they are 'Ignorant Ones', or *Juhhal*. The women, wearing long dresses of dark blue or black and a fine, white veil over their heads, sit in one part of the meeting-room, while the men sit in another.

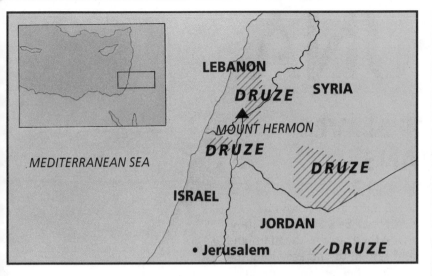

## Knowledgeable Ones

'There's our uncle who is an 'Uqqal.' Samir whispered. 'He looks so dignified with his white turban. That's a symbol of purity. He has to live a much stricter life than our parents. He mustn't drink wine or smoke tobacco. He sometimes eats with us, but he always checks that we've bought or grown the food ourselves. He wouldn't eat it if he thought we'd stolen it. When village matters have been discussed at the meeting, all the *Juhhal* will leave and our parents will come home. But our uncle will stay with the *'Uqqal* for secret meditation and to learn more about Druze beliefs.'

## Lessons to learn

All the children in a Druze village go to the meeting-hall, where they're taught how they must live. They learn that they must not tell others about their beliefs, and must never believe in anything else, such as Islam or Christianity. They're told that it's important to be honest and truthful, particularly to other Druze.

## DO YOU KNOW?

The Druze scriptures, or 'Book of Wisdom', are written by hand. They are guarded carefully and in secret, and only 'Knowledgeable Ones' are allowed to study them.

## You Can Pray for the Druze

### Dear Lord Jesus

1 Help the Druze to understand that only you can make them really honest and truthful.

2 Please show children like Samir and Salim that studying the secret beliefs of the Druze will never help them to know you.

3 May Christians make friends with Druze people, and help them to understand that God wants them to be his friends, too.

4 May many Druze be willing to accept the Bible, to read it and discover that you are God over everything.

5 Send Christians to tell the Druze that you are the true Saviour from God.

6 May Druze children who go to Christian schools learn that you are 'the way, the truth and the life'.

7 Please help the few Druze Christians to stand firm for you. Show them that what you've done is not a secret, but something wonderful that you want them to share with others.

## Caring for strangers

They are taught, too, that they must always be ready to help one another and look after strangers who come for help.

Ali was being hunted by bandits in Syria, but knew that he would find shelter in the chief's home in a Druze village. One day the armed bandits came into the village looking for him. Emad, the chief, walked quietly out to greet them.

'Where is Ali? Give him up to us at once!' the bandits demanded. 'We know he is here. We'll make a deal with him. If he gives us his money he can live!'

'I am a Druze,' Emad replied, 'and to me what you are demanding is disgusting. This man has come to my home for shelter, and I and my village will fight to the death to protect him!'

As the bandits raised their rifles, the villagers fired shots at them. The bandits fled. Emad smiled. He had protected Ali, as his Druze religion demanded.

God longs for the Druze to turn to him and put their trust in Jesus, the Saviour he has sent. He wants them to know that their secret religion and all their beliefs will never bring them to know him. Instead, the Druze go on waiting for Al-Hakim, the founder of their religion, to return to earth as their saviour.

# GARIFUNA

## DESCENDANTS OF SLAVES AND CARIB INDIANS

### Treasure!

The customs official at a small Caribbean airport rummaged through Roger's suitcase. 'What's this?' he demanded, as he pulled out a book. He flicked it open. 'What language is it? It's not Spanish.'

'It's a Garifuna (*Gah-ree-foo-na*) New Testament,' Roger replied.

'Garifuna!' the official exclaimed. 'Why, that's my language! I don't know how to read it, and I've never seen a book in Garifuna before. I've seen a Spanish Bible, but where can I get a copy of this New Testament in Garifuna?'

'I'm afraid they're all sold out,' Roger explained. 'I've only my own copy left.'

'Please let me have it,' the man pleaded. When Roger gave it to him, he danced around the room, clutching the New Testament and shouting for joy, 'Look what I've got! Look what I've got!'

### Shipwrecked slaves

The Garifuna, or Black Caribs, are descendants of slaves brought from Africa in the seventeenth century by British and Spanish boats. Sometimes these boats were shipwrecked and the slaves escaped. Other slaves were set free by their masters. Many of them settled on St. Vincent, in the Windward Islands, where they intermarried with the Carib Indians.

They seem to have been a very unruly and troublesome people, and in 1797 the British shipped them all off to the island of Roatan, far away across the Caribbean Sea. Eventually they made their way to the mainland and settled in villages along the coasts of Belize, Honduras and Guatemala. There many of them still make their living by fishing and farming.

They took with them their own worship of spirits which was soon mixed with Catholicism. Most children are baptized into the Roman Catholic Church, but are protected from evil spirits by a ribbon tied round the wrist. Almost every house has a cross over the doorway to protect the family from harm believed to be caused by the many spirits which they think live all around them. They believe dreams, crying chickens and howling dogs are all omens to foretell the future.

Nearly all the Garifuna speak Spanish, the language of the countries in which they live.

They have their own language, too, which they speak among themselves. Only a few other people have learned to speak it. Now that the New Testament has been translated into Garifuna, work has begun also on the Old Testament. The Jesus film, too, has been dubbed in Garifuna.

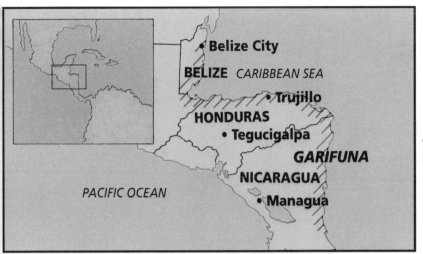

# Jesus is alive!

Two hundred Garifuna people crowded the field outside their village and watched intently as the Jesus film was shown.

'Hello. What are you doing?' Jesus says in Garifuna on the film to a small child. 'Nothing,' was the child's reply.

'He knows our greeting,' the people cried in delight, clapping their hands. 'He knows our language!' Eagerly they watched the film, chatting to one another about what they saw and heard.

'Who wouldn't believe in Jesus?' one lady said to her friend. 'Did you see how he healed the blind man?'

'Look, look!' the men shouted.

'They go fishing like us. We know what it's like to fish all night and catch nothing. He told them to put their nets back in the sea. What a good catch they had then! Amazing! Did you see how Jesus calmed the storm? We all know people who've died in storms like that. He must be more powerful than all the spirits of the sea if he can do that! He must be worth following.'

As they watched the scenes of the crucifixion, many wept, and at the end of the film thirty-five people said they wanted to follow Jesus.

The next night more people came, and even more made decisions to follow him.

God is at work among the Garifuna people. Many of them are hungry to hear God's Word, and are opening their hearts to his love. The churches are growing, as more and more Garifuna trust Jesus for salvation. One Garifuna minister was so delighted with his New Testament that he declared, 'May we chew the Word, swallow it and let it enter into our veins!' Yes, God is working among the Garifuna.

## You Can Pray for the Garifuna

### Dear Lord Jesus

1 Thank you for the Garifuna New Testament. May your Word in their language speak to the hearts of the people.

2 May the Old Testament soon be available. Please use it to teach all who read it more about your care for those who follow you.

3 Give patience to those who hold workshops to help grown-ups and children to read the long and complicated words in their language.

4 Every time the Jesus film is shown please use it to make more Garifunas want to follow you.

5 Help Garifuna Christians to write stories and books which will help their people to understand more about themselves and about your love for them.

6 Please send people to train Garifuna Christians to become pastors, leaders and evangelists who will teach the gospel clearly in their churches.

7 Thank you for each one who has become a Christian. Help them to tell their family and friends how you have changed their lives.

## DO YOU KNOW?

There are about 100,000 Garifuna. Most of them speak Spanish, and some can read it, but Garifuna is the 'language that speaks to their hearts'. At present not many of them can read Garifuna.

# GOND

## FOREST-DWELLERS OF CENTRAL INDIA

### Who can help us?

'What shall we do? There are so many sick people in the village. This illness always brings death. Some have already died, and others are very weak. We've been to the medicine man. He has prayed to the spirits and made sacrifices and offerings to them, but it only seems to make things worse. Why are the spirits treating us like this? What else can we do? Who can help us?'

'Perhaps we should ask the Christians and their teacher,' someone suggested. 'They say their God is more powerful than all our spirits. Perhaps he can stop this sickness.'

The people of Lion village went to the missionary. 'Can you help us?' they asked.

'Yes,' replied the Indian missionary. 'I will pray for you, and so will the Christians in the village. Our God is greater than any other god or spirit. He promises that when we pray to him, he will hear us and answer our prayers. He can heal this sickness.'

As the Indian missionary and the Christians prayed together, God healed ten people in Lion village. 'Now we know that the God of the Christians is greater than the spirits,' they said. 'We will follow him.'

### A forest village

Lion village lies deep in the forests of Central India, and the villagers belong to the Gond tribe. There are many tribal people in India, but the Gond are the largest group of all. Most of them are animists.

They are afraid of evil spirits which, they believe, lie in wait in the fields and forests around their homes, looking for ways to harm them. The Gond make sacrifices and offerings to these spirits, hoping they will leave them alone and let them live their lives in peace.

Many of the Gond who live in the forests work as farmers. They keep some cattle and grow crops such as millet, maize, wheat and beans.

Their homes are usually made from bamboo and timber, with thatch roofs. They are very simple, with only one or two rooms. In one room there will be a few wooden stools and a string hammock or two, and in the kitchen some cooking pots.

Many older people cannot read or write, and, as a result, they are cheated when they sell goods in the towns. The Indian government wants to help them, and now there are many schools where Gond children can study.

# Lion village

Quite a number of the people who live in Lion village are Christians. Would you like to go with the missionary to visit them? There are no roads for cars, so you will have to travel all day in a bullock cart to reach them. The carts do not have springs or comfortable seats, so you might feel quite sore as the cart bumps slowly along over the rough trail. You might prefer to walk, even though it's a long way!

You will have plenty of time to look around. Perhaps you will even see a bear or a tiger on the journey through the forest. When you reach Lion village, you'll be welcomed by the Indian missionary who lives there, and by the Christians. They will be so happy to see you and will soon make you feel at home.

The Gond Christians enjoy singing about Jesus and his love for them. They just love to sing! They are eager, too, to hear more about Jesus.

They will tell you that Jesus has changed their lives and has made them into new people. Jesus has given them peace and joy, and they want other Gonds to know that they do not need to live in fear of the spirits. The Christians of Lion village know this, because it was only Jesus who had power to help them when they were ill.

## Help change the Gond

There are many more Gond villages where the people have never heard of Jesus. Will you change this as you pray for the Gond?

## DO YOU KNOW?

The Gonds have two important gods. They believe one was born six months before the world was created, and the other six months after. They have other gods, and each family has its own god as well.

## You Can Pray for the Gond

### Dear Lord Jesus

1 May the Christians of Lion village always be filled with joy because you love them.

2 Help them to show other Gond people that you are more powerful than all the spirits they fear.

3 Although the Christians of Lion village do not have many belongings, help them to know they are rich because they belong to you.

4 May many more Gond come to know that you love them and will always be ready to help them.

5 Thank you for the Indian missionaries who work among the Gond. Please keep them safe as they travel the rough trails to reach the villages in the forests.

6 May your Holy Spirit help the missionaries to teach your Word clearly so that more Gond will want to follow you.

7 Bless those who are translating the Bible into Gondi.

# HAZARA

## DESCENDANTS OF THE MONGOL HORDE

Almost 800 years ago Genghis Khan, the powerful leader of the Mongols, sent his ambassadors into Central Asia. They were not welcome! So Genghis Khan and his mighty Mongol horde invaded Central Asia to punish the ruler for insulting his ambassadors. The Hazara (pronounced *Ha-zar-a*) claim they are descendants of that Mongol army, and it is not difficult to believe that. With their slanted eyes and round, flat faces they look like Mongolians. Even their language, Hazaragi, has many Mongol words.

Other invaders came, and the Hazara were pushed further and further into the high mountains of Afghanistan. The region they live in is called Hazarajat.

### Life in Hazarajat

The Hazara live in small houses built of mud bricks, and in the hot summer months they dry mulberries, grapes and peaches on the flat roofs. A good stock of food for the long, cold winters is very important. No one likes to be hungry! Wealthier people live in large houses, which look like walled fortresses. It must be noisy in the courtyard, because all the animals belonging to the family live there: dogs, donkey, goats, sheep, hens and even the cow.

A few years ago I visited Pakistan and met Abdul*, a Hazara refugee. 'What is it like to live in Hazarajat?' I asked him.

Abdul smiled. 'Sometimes I think of the summer months,' he replied, 'when we took our sheep and goats up to the high valleys in the mountains where

* Not his real name.

there is plenty of pasture. We had to look after the flock very carefully, and often had to drive away wolves and eagles when they tried to snatch the smaller animals. While we were there we lived in *yurts* (tents) made from reed mats. The women and girls churned the milk. Some of it they used to make balls of *crut* (hard cheese) for the winter.

'The winters are very cold, and for six months the snow is deep. We call it "Afghan gold", because often the snow is our only source of water. Without it our crops fail and we starve.'

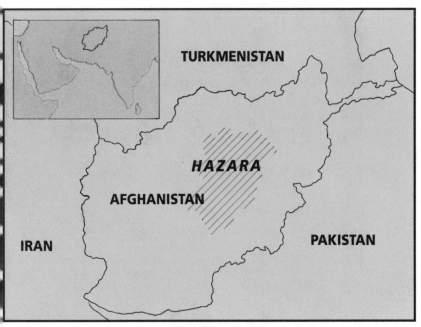

TURKMENISTAN

AFGHANISTAN

*HAZARA*

IRAN

PAKISTAN

## A refugee

'Why did you leave Afghanistan?' I asked.

'In my own country we are looked down on,' Abdul told me. 'Some Hazara live in the cities, where they have to do the hardest work for very little money. It is only right that we should want a better life. In 1979 thousands of Hazara demonstrated against the government. Many Hazara were taken prisoner and have never been heard of since.

'A year later the Soviet troops arrived. They burned our houses and fields. The *mujahidin*, who were Muslim soldiers, were also fighting for power. There was not much left for us to live for. My father was afraid I would be killed. He told me to go across the mountains to Pakistan with other refugees. He wanted me to keep on studying.'

Abdul looked all round and came closer. 'I studied English,' he said, 'because I knew that would help me get a good job. It did, and I started work in a hospital. Soon I was invited to join an English club. There I learnt about Jesus, the Son of God. He loves even the most despised people, the homeless and poor, and that means he loves the Hazara.' Abdul moved even closer. 'I am a follower of Jesus,' he whispered. 'If the *mujahidin* knew that they would kill me. Please pray for me.'

A few months later Abdul returned to Hazarajat. He and several other new Christians in Pakistan had been betrayed. The *mujahidin* were hunting for him.

When I remember Abdul, I am reminded of the church in Smyrna. It was very hard to live there as a Christian, and some were martyred for their faith. 'Be faithful, even if you have to die,' Jesus told them. Will you pray that God will keep Abdul and other Hazara Christians faithful to him always?

## You Can Pray for the Hazara

### Dear Lord Jesus

1 Please keep Hazara Christians, such as Abdul, faithful to you, especially when life is hard for them.

2 Use Christian aid workers in Afghanistan to show Hazara people that they are important to you.

3 Protect Christian aid workers who are helping those who have been hurt in the fighting in Afghanistan.

4 Help Hazara Christians to be bold in sharing their faith with others.

5 Send Christians to encourage the Hazara refugees living in Pakistan, far from their homes and families.

6 As most Hazara people know Dari, help those Christians who have a Dari New Testament to read and understand it.

7 Use Christian radio programmes in Dari to speak to the Hazara people. May programmes be made in Hazaragi, too.

# HUI

## CHINESE DESCENDANTS OF WARRIORS AND MERCHANTS FROM ARABIA

A few years ago I visited some friends who live in a city in north central China. 'Come and eat *momo* (dumplings) with us,' they invited, 'or perhaps you would prefer *lamien* (noodles). We'll go to a nearby Hui (pronounced *'whey'*) restaurant. The food there is very good. Of course the Hui do not eat pork because they are Muslims.'

As we walked along the busy street, I saw people who looked like most Chinese people I'd ever met. They had black hair, and similar faces. They wore the same kind of clothes, but something was different. The men had white caps on their heads, and the women were wearing short veils of fine black, or dark green, cloth.

'These are Hui people,' my friends told me. 'They live in this part of the city, near the main mosque. We'll bring you back here on Friday and you will see how many hundreds of men come to the mosque to pray and listen to the sermon. They come by bus, by bike, by taxi and on foot.

'Quite recently the Muslims held a big demonstration here. They were protesting about a picture which had been published in a Chinese comic in Taiwan. It showed Muslims praying, and there was a pig with them. That was a great insult to them, and the Muslims here were very angry and protested about it.'

# Learning Arabic

Liang is a Hui boy. His father goes to the mosque every Friday. He has even been on pilgrimage (*hajj*) to Mecca. 'Sometimes I go to watch the men pray,' Liang said. 'I don't think I want to go to the mosque with them yet, because not many boys and young men go. I'm quite happy to follow our other Islamic customs, though.

'My father wants me to learn Arabic, because that is the language of the Koran. We use some Arabic words when we talk together at home, but he wants me to read it. There are Arabic words on the walls of the mosque. They look very beautiful, but I think it will be a difficult language to learn. At present I am learning to write Chinese. That is difficult, too!'

Right now there are very few Hui Christians, perhaps no more than twenty altogether. The Hui hold tightly to their traditions, and probably only a quarter of them have ever heard the truth about Jesus. How will they hear about the Saviour who loves them and wants them to follow him? Who will tell them?

## Merchants and warriors

Who are the Hui? Where did they come from and why are they Muslims?

More than a thousand years ago hundreds of Arab and Persian merchants made the long journey along the silk road, right across Asia to China. Arab warriors came to China to help Chinese emperors fight against their enemies. Still more Arabs arrived in China by sea. Many of them never returned to their homelands.

These men were Muslims, and proud of their Arab background. Wherever they settled in China, they built mosques, married local Chinese women and brought their children up as Muslims. They became known as the Hui.

You will find Hui Muslims scattered right across China. In the countryside they often work as farmers. In towns and cities they live around their mosques. They have their own shops and restaurants. They work as butchers, truck drivers and as merchants of leather and gems. Some are teachers, doctors, dentists or engineers.

In many parts of China the Hui seem no different from the Han, who are the people we usually think of as Chinese. They speak Mandarin. They have Chinese names and look and dress like them. But they are different. They are Muslims.

There are more than eight and a half million Hui in China. So many of them live in north-central China that the Chinese government has set up a special region for them. This is called the Ningxia (pronounced *Ning-shia*) Hui Autonomous Region. About a third of the people who live in the region are Hui. There they can follow their own religion and culture.

## You Can Pray for the Hui

### Dear Lord Jesus

1 Please show the Hui children and young people that keeping their traditions, customs and laws will never bring them salvation.

2 Speak to them through dreams and visions of your love, power and gift of salvation.

3 Help those preparing Christian radio programmes for Hui people, to make them so interesting that people will be eager to listen to them.

4 May Hui people who are seeking the truth listen to the programmes and find you as 'the way, the truth and the life'.

5 Use Christian literature, whether it is given to them or sent from abroad, to bring Hui people to trust in you.

6 When a Christian meets a Hui, help them to show your great love, so that the Hui person will see you and not the Christian.

7 Call many people to pray for the Hui and to take the gospel to them.

# KYRGYZ

## WHO LIVE IN A LAND OF SNOW-CAPPED MOUNTAINS

Aigul, whose name means 'moon beauty', sat staring through the classroom window at the high, snow-capped Tien Shan mountains. 'How beautiful they are,' she thought. 'They deserve to be called the Heavenly Mountains.' Beyond the mountains is north-west China.

### A Kyrgyz hero

Aigul's teacher had just been telling the class an exciting story about Manas, an ancient Kyrgyz hero. Aigul had already learned many legends, poems and songs about Manas.

Manas was only a baby in his cradle when he began to talk, and almost before he could walk he learned to ride powerful horses. What a great champion he was on the battlefield! He was only nine years old when he freed his father and tribe from their enemies. Soon he became leader of all the nomadic tribes who wandered across that part of Central Asia.

Nobody really knows whether the stories about Manas are true, but the Kyrgyz proudly remember him as their hero. Even the local airport is named after him.

Bishkek, where Aigul lives, is the capital of Kyrgyzstan (pronounced *Ker-ger-stan*), a small, Muslim republic in Central Asia. It is a modern city with broad, tree-lined streets and colourful parks and gardens. Kyrgyzstan became a part of the Soviet Union in 1930. German and Russian Christians lived there, but very few Kyrgyz had ever heard of Jesus. In 1990 Kyrgyzstan declared independence, and Christians from other countries came to help the churches, and to tell Kyrgyz about God's love for them.

### Shepherds and sheep

Only a hundred years ago the Kyrgyz were nomads. They wandered from pasture to pasture in the valleys of the Tien Shan mountains with their herds of sheep, goats, yaks and camels. They lived in *yurts*, which are like round tents made from thick, heavy felt. In the centre of the Kyrgyz flag is the symbol of the top of a *yurt*, to remind them of their history.

There are two and a half times as many sheep in Kyrgyzstan as there are people, because every Kyrgyz family is expected to own a cow and a few sheep and goats. Several families join together to employ a shepherd to look after their animals. He leads the flock from pasture to pasture, just as his father and grandfather did. It's not surprising that sheep are another important symbol of Kyrgyz life.

## DO YOU KNOW?

The Kyrgyz have many proverbs and sayings. Here is one: 'It is the fly between two fighting camels that gets the worst of it!'

## Feasts

There's always plenty of mutton to eat, too. Their national dish, called '*besh-barmak*', is made from mutton mixed with noodles. Its name means 'five fingers'. Why? Because the Kyrgyz used to eat it with their hands.

When people in Kyrgyzstan receive very good news, or recover from an operation, they want to show *Kudai* (their god) that they are thankful. They will kill a sheep, because blood must be shed to show their gratitude. Then they will share the meat with their family and friends in a special thanksgiving meal.

At the feast, the sheep's head is presented to the guest of honour. He has to carve it up and give different parts to each guest. 'This eye is for you,' he says. 'Eat it, so your sight will improve!' To the youngest guest of all he gives an ear saying, 'This is to remind you to listen to your elders!' These feasts are happy times, especially if a story-teller is there who can tell exciting tales of Manas and his brave deeds.

As Aigul thought about Manas, she remembered

another hero she had heard about the week before. Two teachers from the U.S.A. had come to their school and had told them stories about Jesus, God's Son. Aigul had listened eagerly to the stories.

'Fancy God sending his only son to be born as a baby,' she said to herself. 'He grew up to be such a good, kind man. It was sad that cruel men hated him so much that they crucified him.' As Aigul remembered the stories about Jesus she thought, 'How different Jesus is from Manas. Why, Manas died a long time ago, but even though Jesus died, the teachers say he rose from the dead and is alive today!'

## You Can Pray for the Kyrgyz

### Dear Lord Jesus

1 Now that Christians in Kyrgyzstan are free to tell others about their faith, please give them courage to speak boldly about you.

2 Please protect the few Kyrgyz Christians from those who would harm them because they are now following you.

3 Help all the local Christians, whether they are Kyrgyz, Russian, German or from some other country, to work together in love.

4 Please send more Christians to witness in country areas where most people have never heard about you.

5 May many Kyrgyz boys and girls hear about you and come to know you for themselves.

6 Thank you for the Kyrgyz New Testament. May your Holy Spirit help Kyrgyz Christians to understand and obey what they read in it.

7 May many people buy books from the new Christian bookshop, which will help them to follow you.

# MANDINKA

## WHO RELY ON CHARMS TO KEEP THEM SAFE

### Charms for her baby

Nene cuddled her baby son. Outside her mud-and-thatch house the village people were singing and dancing. The *marabout* (Muslim teacher) had come, and Nene had paid him to tie ten *jujus* (charms) around Oumar's arms, neck and waist. She hoped these would keep him safe from sickness and evil spirits, and bring him good luck. Nene sighed. The charms hadn't worked for her other three babies. They had all become sick and died. Nene had wanted to take the children to the Christian nurse at the nearby clinic, but her husband wouldn't let her. 'They will make you take off the *jujus* and burn them,' he told her, 'then the children will have no protection from the evil spirits. We have to follow our Mandinka ways.'

The *marabout* makes *jujus* from pieces of paper which have the name of a demon and a verse from the Koran written on them. The *jujus* are sewn into little leather pouches and hung on a string. The people believe these *jujus* are very powerful, and that the power comes from Allah, the Muslim God.

### Followers of Islam

Almost half the people living in the small West African country of Gambia are Mandinkas. Many centuries ago they left their homeland in Mali and

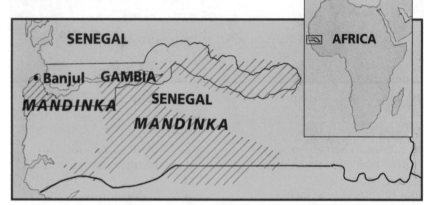

travelled west in search of better farmland. Eventually they settled in Gambia and the surrounding countries.

The Mandinkas were animists. Some became Muslims, converted by traders who passed through the region, but most of them continued to follow their own traditional religion.

Later the Muslims forced the Mandinkas to follow Islam. Now most Mandinkas say they are Muslims, but many of them still believe in their old animist religion as well.

## Showing God's love

There are not many Mandinka Christians yet. Missionaries try to show them that God loves them and can set them free from the power and fear of evil spirits.

In Christian hospitals and clinics, doctors and nurses pray for their patients, as well as treating their illnesses. Some missionaries are teaching Mandinka people to read in their own language, and even take special classes in prisons. Others have translated the New Testament into Mandinka. Young people can hear about Jesus in youth centres, and farmers are helped to grow better crops.

Above all the missionaries want the Mandinka to know that if they put their trust in Jesus, they need not be afraid of anything else, because God has conquered all the powers of darkness.

## DO YOU KNOW?

Only two out of every ten Mandinka people can read, so programmes to teach them to read are very important.

## You Can Pray for the Mandinka

### Dear Lord Jesus

1 Please help Oumar and other Christians to live in a way that will always please you.

2 Thank you for the Mandinka New Testament. As Christians read it, help them to understand how much you love them and want to help them.

3 Help those who are learning to read. As they learn, may they understand more about your love.

4 May the Muslims who are helping to translate the Old Testament come to know you for themselves.

5 Baboo is an old man who has often heard the gospel but is afraid to follow you. Help him to know that you are the most powerful God of all.

6 Help the Mandinkas who do know you to tell others about your love.

7 Help many Mandinkas to overcome their fear of evil spirits and put their trust in you.

# Who will give me peace?

Oumar was a very frightened little boy. Sometimes, as he sat near the fire at night, he heard grown-ups tell stories about beautiful women who were really witches and sold children for meat. Oumar often had strange dreams, and was scared to go anywhere in the dark.

'Is there a god anywhere who can give me peace and take away my fears?' he wondered. His mother, a Muslim, told him that Allah would help him. He learned all he could from the Muslim teachers. He prayed five times every day and fasted during the month of Ramadan, but he still didn't have peace.

At the Catholic High School Oumar studied hard. He thought this would help him get a good job, so that he could help his mother. There he started to learn about the Lord Jesus Christ, the Son of God. 'I wonder which is true?' he asked himself. 'Is it the way of Islam, or is it the way of Christ?'

As time went on Oumar began a Bible Correspondence Course. He wanted to prove that Jesus Christ was not really the Son of God. To his surprise, he found that he was learning about a God who loves men and women, and can take away their fears. Now, more than anything, Oumar wanted to belong to this God, but he was afraid his mother would be very angry. That night, as he rode home from school, Oumar heard God speak to him. 'You know the truth now, but what are you going to do about it?'

The next day Oumar told his teacher that he wanted to give his life to the Lord Jesus. Now Oumar knows that Jesus is always with him and has taken away all his fears.

# NEWAR

## OF NEPAL, THE ONLY HINDU KINGDOM IN THE WORLD

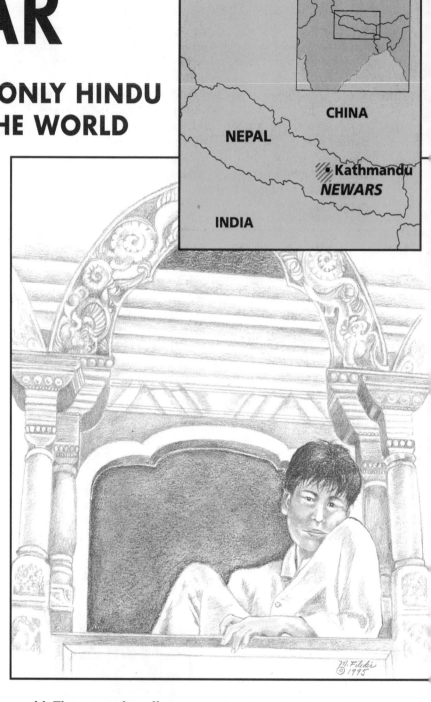

The kingdom of Nepal is a beautiful, fascinating country. The majestic, snow-covered peaks of the Himalayas, including Mount Everest, form its northern border with China. Only a hundred miles to the south the Terai, Nepal's border with India, is flat and fertile. There you can find the Royal Chitwan National Park, famous for its elephants, rhinoceros and tigers.

### Many different peoples

Nepal is home to almost a hundred different people groups, who live in villages along deep river valleys, or on the sides of mountains. There are few roads, and goods are carried into these villages on the backs of men or donkeys along rough and narrow trails.

In the fertile Kathmandu Valley the people grow rice, corn, wheat and many different kinds of fruit and vegetables. The cities of Kathmandu, Patan and Bhaktapur are full of ancient Hindu temples and shrines, huge Buddhist *stupas* (shrines), and many beautiful houses and palaces, with carved wooden doors and shutters. Visiting these cities is like visiting a huge, open-air museum.

### A Hindu kingdom

Nepal is proud of being the only Hindu kingdom in the world, but in fact its Hinduism is mixed with Buddhism and Animism. In 1816, after a war with the British in India over the Terai, Nepal shut itself off from the rest of the world. They started to allow foreigners to visit again in 1951. Christian organizations were among those who wanted to help the new King and his country. Some Nepalis became Christians, but were often put in prison. Only since 1991 have Christians really been free to follow their faith.

All this time Nepalis who lived outside Nepal were hearing about Jesus. Many people were praying that one day the gospel could be taught in Nepal. Now there are more than 50,000 Christians in Nepal! There are still many more towns and scattered villages where men and women have not yet heard of the love of God.

# The Living Goddess

'I wonder what it must be like to be Kumari, the Living Goddess,' Maya wondered. 'She is a Newari girl, and is always chosen from the gold and silver-smiths' caste. She has to be perfect, and is only five years old when she's chosen. The many tests she has to pass sound so frightening. She wears beautiful clothes and jewels and lives in Kathmandu, in Kumari Bahal, the House of the Living Goddess.

People worship her, and even the king comes to her for advice. How strange it will be for her when she reaches her teens and becomes an ordinary person again!'

Kumari is only a goddess for about ten years. Jesus is so different! He is God for ever, and has always been God. What's more, he promises he will always be with those who follow him. Will you pray that Maya, and many other Newars, will come to know Jesus, the eternal Son of the one true living God?

## You Can Pray for Nepal and the Newar

### Dear Lord Jesus

1 Thank you that there are now Christians in Nepal. Help them to tell their families, friends and neighbours about you.

2 May Newari children hear about you, and learn that you are the living God, not just another god to worship.

3 When Newars come to know you, help them to discover that you are more powerful than all the many gods they worship.

4 Help Christian tourists visiting the interesting cities of Kathmandu, Patan and Bhaktapur to share their faith with the Newars they meet.

5 Thank you that Christian literature can be given out freely. Please use every gospel tract and leaflet to bring at least one person to know you.

6 Bring many university students to know you, especially those who will help govern their country in the future.

7 Call out Christians who are willing to take the gospel to the Newar, and to every other people group in Nepal.

## A Newari girl's story

The Newar, who live in the Kathmandu Valley, are Buddhists, but Hinduism is strongly mixed in with their beliefs.

Maya, a Newari girl living in the city of Bhaktapur, picked up the heavy brass water pot and glanced round the room. It was lit by the early morning light filtering through the beautiful, carved window screen. She had already helped her mother to sweep the floors in the house.

She joined some other girls going to the water tank. Chattering, they passed several temples where people were worshipping and making their offerings to the gods. On they went, through the potters' square. The potters were already busy throwing new pots on their wheels. At the water tank, Maya washed herself then filled her brass water pot.

As she went back into her home, Maya glanced up at the figure of Ganesh, the Hindu elephant god, who, the Newars believe, brings wealth and wisdom to their homes.

'We have gods everywhere,' she thought as she started to help her mother prepare the offerings of vermilion powder, rice and flower petals for the Buddha and the other gods in their house and at the temple. 'We have gods for every part of our lives. My friends and I are were even married to Vishnu when we were little girls so that we can never become widows.'

# NORTH AFRICANS
## IN FRANCE

## NOT AT HOME IN FRANCE, NO LONGER AT HOME IN AFRICA

### Who am I?

'Where do I belong?' nine-year-old Youssef muttered to himself as he kicked a Pepsi can along the gutter. 'I was born in France, I speak French, I go to a French school and wear the same kind of clothes as any other French boy. I'm tired of being teased about being a "Beur"* in school, and told to go home to Algeria.

'When my mother used to take me to visit her family in Algeria, I didn't like it at all. Everything seemed so strange and a bit frightening. I can't speak Arabic, so I couldn't even talk with my cousins or grandparents. I don't belong there!'

### Workers

After the Second World War, many Algerians came to work in France. When Youssef's father arrived in the 1960s, he found work as a labourer on a building site. Soon his wife joined him. Now they have six children, and live in a small, overcrowded flat in an over-crowded suburb of Paris, where thousands of other immigrant families from North Africa make their homes.

There are almost three and a half million North Africans living in France. Most of them

are Muslims, and many of the older immigrants try to live in exactly the same way as they did in the countries they came from. It helps them to feel secure in a country where many people do not want them. Their children, like Youssef, think of themselves as French, and do not want to follow the ways of their parents. They are confused, and often do not know where they really belong.

There's very little work for the North Africans at present, because there is so much unemployment in France. 'Beurs go home! Muslims out! Out!' has become a familiar cry.

* Beur – a person born in France to North African parents.

94

## Youssef's family

'My father goes to the mosque and prays sometimes,' says Youssef. 'He tells me he used to pray five times a day when he lived in Algeria. He went to the mosque every Friday. When he came to France, he worked with some French people who tried to tell him there is no God. He found that strange, because he always thought France was a Christian country. When I ask him about God, he doesn't want to answer my questions. I wonder if he is as sure about him as he used to be.

'My brothers don't go to the mosque or pray, but my parents say my sister must wear a headscarf in school. Actually, my sister is quite glad that the education minister has banned headscarves, because she doesn't want to look different from her French friends. Out of doors my mother still wears a veil which covers her from head to foot.'

## Bible club

One Wednesday afternoon, which is a school holiday in France, Youssef wandered along the street wondering what to do. A lady invited him to come to a children's club in a local church. He felt very shy, but the other children made him feel at home, and no one teased him about being a Beur. Soon he joined in singing the happy songs. Then there was a wonderful story from the Bible. How he enjoyed it! 'Did Jesus really love children like that?' Youssef wondered. 'I'm going back to the club each week!'

One of the lady helpers at the children's club began to visit Youssef's mother to teach her to read and write in French. They read the same stories from the Bible that Youssef learnt at the children's club. A man from the church met Youssef's father and invited him to their coffee bar.

Normally Youssef's parents wouldn't go to a church, because they are Muslims, but now they have made a few friends there they feel much happier. No one makes fun of them because they are Algerians and don't speak French very well. Besides, they talk about important things such as how to know God and belong to his family.

Will you pray that Youssef and his family, and many more North Africans like them, who feel they do not belong anywhere, will become God's people? God wants to be their special friend and he wants them to belong to his family.

### DO YOU KNOW?

There are only about 1,000 Christians among the 3,500,000 North Africans living in France.

## You Can Pray for North Africans in France

### Dear Lord Jesus

1 Help the few North African Christians in France to stand firm for you, even when their own people try to force them to return to Islam.

2 May Christians make friends with North Africans and show them that you care for them, even when others despise and hate them.

3 Send Christians to help Beur children to understand that you are their true friend and want them to belong to your family.

4 May the truth of the songs and Bible stories that Beur children learn in children's clubs go right into their minds and hearts.

5 When North Africans pray in their mosques in France, please show them that only you can give them true hope and security.

6 Give courage to North Africans to take Christian leaflets from the bookstalls in markets and universities, and even to buy Bibles and books.

7 Please send Christians who can speak Arabic as well as French, so that they can talk to the older women who often don't know much French.

95

# PYGMIES

## SMALL HUNTERS OF THE GREAT ITURI FOREST

### Hunting in the forest

'Soon you can come hunting with us!'

Mateke tried to hide his excitement. Every arrow he had shot that morning had hit the tree-stump target. He and his friend Matedu often practised shooting at big spiders, rats and even frogs. 'How soon,' Mateke wondered, 'will it be before I really can hunt with the men, instead of gathering fruit and nuts, leaves and grubs and looking after my small brother?'

Mateke joined the other children to watch the men of the village as they got ready to go hunting. They had sharpened their arrows. Now they were preparing poison from the bark of the *anga* tree. Carefully, one of the men dipped the tip of each arrow into the poison. The men took their arrows and dried them over the embers of the fire.

The time came to start out. Two or three women glided out of the clearing into the forest. The men followed silently. The giant trees towered high above them, shutting out the sunlight. Vines looped down from the branches. Huge, twisted roots, creepers and young trees tangled for space on the ground.

The women had made beaters from the strong stems and leaves of the *mangunga* plant. Their job was to beat the ground, calling out to frighten the animals and make them run towards the hunters. What would the men catch today? Would it be monkeys, or birds or a deer?

### Elbow high

Mateke is a Pygmy. The name 'pygmy' comes from a Greek word which means 'elbow high', and a true adult pygmy stands only about 1.35 metres tall. They live in the tropical rain forests of central Africa, so it is not surprising that they call themselves the 'children of the forest'. Mateke's tribe lives in the great Ituri forest of north-east Zaire.

Mateke's mouth watered as he thought of the delicious stew his mother would make.

### New huts

Mateke looked round his village. There were only five huts in the village. He had heard the men say it would soon be time to move again, for there was not much food left for them in that part of the forest.

Each time they move, the Pygmies collect their few belongings – their bows and arrows, knives and cooking pots – and move off into the forest. When they have found a good place, the men make a fresh clearing. The women build new huts of long, thin branches, bent to form a small dome. They thatch the dome with large *mangunga* leaves, leaving a small opening for a door. The pygmy huts have no furniture. All they need is a mattress made of *mangunga* leaves!

## God's Book

'When we move do you think old Bamata will find us again?' Mateke asked Matedu. 'I hope he will. He tells such interesting stories about the God who made us. Do you remember how we all hid in the forest the first time he came, because we were afraid of him?'

'Yes, and he brought us salt, which is so useful. Did you hear what he asked my father?' Matedu said. 'He asked him if he ever prayed to God.'

'And your father said he did,' replied Mateke. 'He told Bamata that the forest is our god. He said it is our father and mother and gives us all we need. It gives us our houses, food and clothing, and when a big storm comes it protects us.'

'Bamata showed my father something which he called "God's Book". He told him that the Book says there is one God,' Matedu smiled, 'and that he made our forest, the trees, the animals and even us. Bamata said that we have all offended God, but, because he wants us to follow him, he sent his Son called Jesus. He died for all of us, and if we ask him to forgive us, he will. Then we can follow him. My father says his heart tells him this is true.'

In the remote Ituri forest of Zaire, and in other parts of Central Africa, Pygmies are becoming Christians. Zaireans and Pygmy evangelists are telling them about the love of God, but there are many who still need to hear about him.

## You Can Pray for the Pygmies

### Dear Lord Jesus

1 Please show the evangelists ways to tell Pygmies the gospel so that they will understand it clearly.

2 Send evangelists who will be ready to live and travel in the forests with the Pygmies and teach them more about you.

3 Help the evangelists to learn the Pygmy languages, so that the Pygmies will understand what they say more easily.

4 Help those who make cassettes in Pygmy languages to tell the truth about you clearly.

5 When Pygmy children hear about you, help them to trust in you.

6 Help Pygmies not to be afraid of tall strangers who come to tell them about Jesus.

7 Please help the few Pygmies who go to Bible School to cope with things that are new to them, such as walls, beds, reading and writing.

# QASHQA'I

## NOMADS OF IRAN

Ali stirred in his bed on the carpeted floor of his family's tent in the Zagros mountains. It was time to get up. Outside the tent his mother was baking *nan* (flat) bread on a griddle over the fire. She was always up first, and was busy all day long. Quickly, Ali rolled up his bedding and put it carefully on the covered heap of household goods. He was hungry, and fresh bread, cheese and tea are delicious for breakfast.

The Qashqa'i (pronounced *Kash-guy*) people are nomads living in the south of Iran. During winter they live on the coastal plain near the Persian Gulf. There they plant fields, grow fruit and look after their flocks of sheep and goats. In March the weather starts to get hot, and the grass shrivels and dries. Then it is time for them to leave for their summer pastures, high up in the Zagros mountains.

### A long journey

As he ate his breakfast, Ali remembered those busy days back in the village near the coast. The sheep and goats had been shorn and the household goods packed, ready for the long journey. Early one morning the tents were taken down and carefully folded. Soon the tents, bags, boxes and the little children had been tied onto the backs of donkeys and horses and the journey began.

The men and boys walked slowly with their flocks, which fed on the grass as they made their way towards the mountains. Each day they travelled about ten miles, and each evening the men pitched the tents and spread out the carpets and the women cooked the food. The next morning they packed up their tents once more and continued on their journey.

The journey was long and slow, but at last they reached the summer camp. It is much cooler in the mountains than down on the coastal plain, and there is work for everyone to do. Ali and his friends look after the flocks, while their fathers go hunting to make sure there is plenty of food for their families. The girls spin wool and look after the smaller children. When they have finished their daily chores, the women set up their carpet looms and work together, chatting and laughing while they weave their beautiful, colourful carpets.

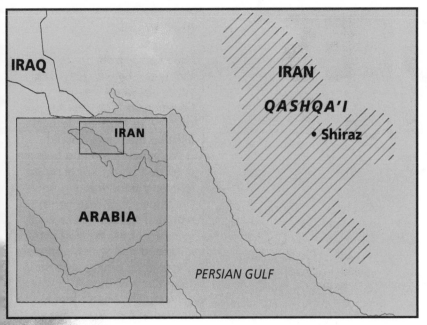

**DO YOU KNOW?**

The Qashqa'i have a saying which sums up their way of life: 'Where my carpet is, there is my home.'

## A tent school

In the evenings the boys and girls go to school in a big, white tent. Ali is glad he can go to school. He is learning to read and write Farsi, the Iranian language, because Qashqa'i is only a spoken language. He hopes that one day he will go to college or university, so that he can become a teacher or doctor among his own Qashqa'i people.

For almost four months the Qashqa'i live in the summer camps. Then the weather starts to get cool, and by the middle of August the nights are very cold, and in the mornings the grass is thick with frost. Once again all the household goods are packed, ready for the long, slow journey back to the warmer south.

Like most people who live in Iran, the Qashqa'i say they are Muslims. When anyone gets married or dies, they like to have a Muslim ceremony, but very few Qashqa'i say their prayers five times a day, or fast during the month of Ramadan.

Sadly, no Christian missionaries have ever gone to tell the Qashqa'i how much Jesus loves them, and now missionaries are not allowed to live in Iran. There are not even any Christian radio broadcasts in the Qashqa'i language. How will the Qashqa'i hear about him? Will children like Ali ever learn about Jesus? Some Qashqa'i people living in the cities of Shiraz and Teheran have heard about Jesus from Christian friends, but only a few have become Christians. Some travel overseas to study. Will they hear about Jesus there?

## You Can Pray for the Qashqa'i

### Dear Lord Jesus

1 Even though missionaries are not allowed to live in Iran, may people in other countries hear about the Qashqa'i and pray for them.

2 Give Christians in Iran courage to show Qashqa'i people they meet how much you love them.

3 May Qashqa'i people who live in Shiraz and Teheran listen to their Christian friends when they tell them about you.

4 When Qashqa'i students go to other countries to study, may they meet Christians who will be kind and helpful to them.

5 May your Holy Spirit work in the hearts of Qashqa'i people who have heard about you, so that they will want to know you for themselves.

6 Use the Christian radio programmes in Farsi to bring Qashqa'i people to yourself.

7 May Qashqa'i people not be afraid to become Christians.

# REFUGEES

## PEOPLE LOOKING FOR HELP AND SAFETY

### Hopelessness

Do you remember seeing pictures on the T.V. of long lines of sad and hopeless refugees from Burundi being turned back on the border with Tanzania? Not long ago there were similar tragic pictures of starving Eritreans, Ethiopians, Somalis and Sudanese, trying to get away from famine and civil war which have haunted their countries. Did you see pictures of refugees fleeing in small boats from the corrupt and brutal regime in Haiti? Or those who left Cuba, hoping they would be allowed to live in the U.S.A? And what about the thousands and thousands of Afghan refugees in Pakistan, proud people whose home is a tent?

### 40 million refugees

At the end of the twentieth century there are about 40 million refugees in the world. That's a staggering number of people. Many of them have been forced to leave their own country because of war or

### Boat People

Mien comes from South Vietnam. She was only five years old when the Communists took over the country. In 1979 her father decided the family should leave because life had become cruel and hard. 'We escaped in a very poor wooden boat,' she remembers. 'We were cramped because there were so many of us. We had very little food and water, and were attacked by pirates who stole everything we had.'

Eventually, Mien's family arrived in Malaysia. 'Even there we weren't wanted, but we were fortunate,' she said. 'Many Vietnamese refugees died when they were attacked or their poor boats sank. At last we were helped, and we came here to live in America. Now I am a teacher, but one day I would like to go back to my own country.'

### Homeless

'I'm so cold, and I'm tired and hungry,' sobbed little Hazir, clutching his mother's skirt. 'When can we stop walking?' His mother looked at him with sadness in her eyes. It was bitterly cold and the snow was falling as they struggled, with hundreds of other Kurds, across the rough mountain pass.

'Not yet,' she replied, gently. 'You must be brave. We've no home now because our home was destroyed by Iraqi bombs. We must go on until we find somewhere safe, someone who will help us. If only we Kurds had a country of our own . . . ' she sighed.

famine, the hatred of one race of people for another, and religious persecution. They are sure they can no longer stay in their own country, for if they did they would suffer great cruelty or even be killed.

Far better, they think, to leave all that they know behind them

## Lost families

'Run, run,' screamed the teacher in a village school in Burundi. 'Get away from here as quickly as you can.' All around them there was fighting. Quickly, the children obeyed.

At home in the village, mothers did not know which way their children had gone, but they, too, fled from the village. Fathers searched for their lost families along the long lines of refugees and in the special camps set up for them in the neighbouring countries of Rwanda, Tanzania and Zaire. Some of them were never found again.

*A Kurdish refugee family flees from persecution.*

and seek a new life somewhere else. But what will that future be?

Some have had to leave their homes and villages for other parts of their own country. People of Croatia, Serbia and Bosnia have fled their homes because of a senseless and terrifying war. Floods in Bangladesh, volcanic eruptions in the Philippines and drought in the Sahel have all caused people to lose their homes. They must look for another place, where they will be safe, have food and care, and be given hope for the future.

## Jesus, a refugee

There have always been refugees. History is full of them. In the Bible, in the book of Exodus, we read about the Israelites fleeing from their harsh slavery in Egypt. Jesus, himself, with Joseph and Mary, were refugees when they fled to Egypt from cruel King Herod.

The Bible tells us that we must care for the poor, the suffering and the refugees. In Matthew 25:34-40 Jesus tells us that those who feed the hungry, give water to the thirsty, provide clothes for those who have none, who look after the sick and visit those in prison, have done all these things for him.

Will you pray for refugees around the world? Ask God to send people to help them, people with hearts full of love, who can tell them of God, who promises to 'wipe away every tear from their eyes'.

## You Can Pray for Refugees

### Dear Lord Jesus

1 Please call many Christians to help the millions of sad and hurting refugees.

2 Send gentle, caring people who can look after babies and small children who are too tiny, ill and weak to help themselves.

3 Some children feel very lonely and unwanted because their parents have died, or have lost them. Help them to know that you are their special friend.

4 Thank you for Christians in countries such as Zaire who have given their love and care to help refugees from Rwanda and Burundi. May their love bring comfort to them.

5 Help us to remember all refugees around the world, especially those who have to live in camps, and don't have homes or enough food or money.

6 Please bring peace to all the troubled areas of the world, so that many refugees can return to their own countries and live without fear.

7 May refugees who get permission to live in the rich countries of the world find people who will be kind to them and help them.

# ROHINGYA

## MUSLIMS IN A BUDDHIST LAND

### Banished!

'Come on. Let's get away from here. There's nowhere left for us to live, now that our home has been burned down.' Marfat Islam looked down at his weeping wife and baby son. There were tears in his own eyes.

'Others from the village are planning to walk across the border into Bangladesh. We'll go with them. The people in Bangladesh are Muslims, too, so perhaps they will help us, even though they are as poor as we are.'

Marfat helped his wife to her feet and picked up his son. There was nothing else to carry. They joined the group of villagers and started to walk through the night. As they made their way along the trail to the border, they spoke quietly of what had happened to them. Their voices were full of fear.

'The soldiers kicked me so much I thought I would die.'

'Me, too. Some of them forced us out of our house, and stole everything we had.'

'They beat me, then took all our rice.'

'A group of soldiers burned down our house and we've lost everything.'

Each person had a similar tale to tell. 'Why can't they leave us alone?' they asked one another. 'After all, we Rohingyas have lived here for many generations, but they say, "You Muslims do not belong in Burma, so you must go to your own land".'

### What would you do?

How would you like it if you were beaten, kicked and forced out of your home, and everything you had was taken from you? What would you do if the government of your country passed a law which meant you no longer belonged in the country where you had been born? Your parents and grand-parents, even your great-grandparents and their ancestors had lived in that country for hundreds of years. What would you do?

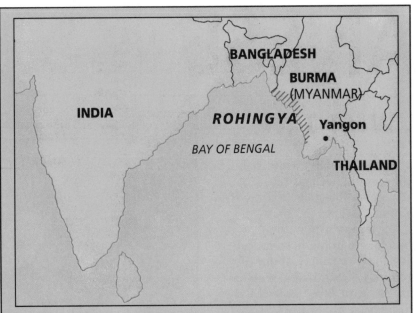

INDIA
BANGLADESH
BURMA (MYANMAR)
ROHINGYA
BAY OF BENGAL
Yangon
THAILAND

# DO YOU KNOW?

Although the Rohingya settled in the Arakan Province of Myanmar more than a thousand years ago, the government of the country says they are not true Burmese.

## You Can Pray for the Rohingya

### Dear Lord Jesus

1 Please bring help to the Rohingya refugees in Bangladesh who have fled from their homeland.

2 Comfort them, especially the children, who are often afraid, sick and hungry.

3 May missionaries and Christian aid-workers in Bangladesh find ways to help the refugees.

4 May Rohingya people who live in Myanmar meet Christians who will show them your love and tell them about you.

5 Lead some of them into Christian churches where they will hear your Word.

6 May the Government of Myanmar change its laws so that the Rohingya can live in the region which has been their home for a thousand years.

7 Change the hearts of the soldiers and make them less harsh in the way they treat the Rohingya people.

# Refugees

In 1978 the government set up a campaign called Operation Dragon King, in an effort to drive the Rohingya out of Burma. Thousands of people fled with their few poor possessions across the border into Bangladesh, on foot, or in rowing-boats along the coast. There they set up flimsy shelters for their families.

But Bangladesh is a poor country, and has troubles enough of its own. It could not look after all these refugees, and sent them back to Burma. There they were still unwanted and persecuted.

Thousands still flee to Bangladesh in their search for a place of peace. Some return to Burma; some stay in Bangladesh, living in makeshift camps; some organize resistance and try to fight back, but without much success.

Most Rohingyas know very little of the gospel, in fact many have never heard of Jesus. Who will tell them the Good News about Jesus? Will those who are refugees in Bangladesh hear the gospel there? Will the church in Myanmar try to help them?

As I read about the Rohingyas, I am reminded of the words in the Bible: 'This world is not our home; we are looking forward to our everlasting home in heaven' (Hebrews 13:14, GNB). Can we pray that someone will tell the Rohingya that God welcomes them and has a special home for them in heaven?

## Room only for Burmese

The Rohingyas, who live in the province of Arakan in Myanmar (as Burma is now called), are Muslims. They are descendants of Arab traders and Muslim preachers who settled in Arakan a thousand years ago and set up their own Muslim state. Two hundred years ago Arakan was overrun by Burma, and then became a part of the British Empire.

When Burma became independent in 1947, the Rohingyas decided to fight for freedom from Burmese rule. The powerful Burmese military government had other ideas! They decided that Burma was to be a Buddhist country and wanted Arakan for themselves. There was no room for the Muslim Rohingya people, or for any other people who were not 'true Burmese'.

# SUNDANESE

## FROM BEAUTIFUL WEST JAVA

### Can the gods help?

'Why do I always seem to forget everything I've learned?' Paru wondered. 'I can never remember the passages from the Koran that I have to learn. I feel so stupid. Even my little brother learns them more easily than I do.'

As Paru wandered up the path between the steeply-terraced rice fields, he gazed upwards at the high volcanic mountains. 'It's no wonder we call the mountains the "home of the gods",' he thought, 'and the gods look after us, too. They must have been pleased with the offerings we made before we planted our fields this year. The rice, corn, tea and hot peppers are all growing so well. I wonder if they would help me to remember those verses from the Koran?'

There are thirty million Sundanese living in beautiful West Java. Paru is just one of millions of Sundanese who have never heard about Jesus. Most Sundanese are Muslims, but, long before they became Muslims, they worshipped their own gods. When Hinduism and Buddhism reached Java from India in the 5th and 6th centuries A.D., they began to worship the gods of those religions as well. Even now that they are Muslims, they continue to worship the gods whose home is in the mountains.

### Christian villages

When the Dutch colonized Java in the nineteenth century, the Sundanese certainly did not want them to be their masters. A few missionaries tried to help the Sundanese, and set up clinics, schools and churches, although the Dutch government did not want them there. The Sundanese did not want them, either, nor did they want to hear about Christianity, because it was the religion of the Dutch, who were hated so much.

When a Sundanese became a Christian, he or she was often persecuted by the Muslims. As a result, the missionaries built special villages for the new Christians. Some of these villages still exist, but nowadays Muslims live in them as well. Sadly, the Christians have little interest in their Muslim neighbours.

About 12,000 Sundanese call themselves Christians, but very few of them really know what it means to have their lives changed by the living Lord Jesus. Most of them belong to the Pasundan churches, which were set up by those early Dutch missionaries.

## DO YOU KNOW?

Although the Sundanese are Muslims, magic plays an important part in Sundanese life, especially in healing and in foretelling the future.

## You Can Pray for the Sundanese

### Dear Lord Jesus

1 Use the Christian Sundanese drama and music programmes to show people that they can be Christians as well as Sundanese.

2 Help the Christians to be strong and trust you, even when people say hurtful things about them.

3 Please send Christians to the villages to tell children, like Paru, that you are more powerful than all the gods in the mountains.

4 May your Holy Spirit give the Christians of the Pasundan churches courage and power to witness to their Muslim neighbours.

5 Help Christians to want to read the Bible, and may your Holy Spirit help them to understand it.

6 Help those who are preparing radio programmes to make them really interesting and show clearly what it means to be a Christian.

7 May many more people around the world take an interest in the Sundanese and pray for them.

# Music and drama

'How can we show the Sundanese that Christianity is not a Western religion, but is for everyone?' Christians from other parts of Indonesia are asking themselves. So they have set up their own mission. 'We'll use Sundanese drama and music to tell them Bible stories. This will help them understand that Sundanese can become Christians, too!'

One evening, as Sita and her friends were walking along a busy street in Jakarta, the capital of Java, two young people stopped them. 'Come and watch the story of why God in heaven sent his only Son to earth,' they invited Sita and her friends.

'What a wonderful story,' said Sita afterwards, 'and it was so easy to understand, because it was just like our Sundanese plays. The Christians' God must be really powerful to be able to bring his Son back to life again after he was killed. I would like to know more about him.'

God was working in Sita's heart. Some months later she became a Christian, and her family were very angry with her. 'What do you mean, you've become a Christian?' shouted her brother. 'You cannot be a Christian! We Sundanese are Muslims.' Sita was sad, but she knew she must go on following her Saviour.

The Sundanese are one of the largest unreached people groups in the world. Will you pray that more Christians will go to live and work among the Sundanese, and will find interesting ways of showing the them that God cares for them and wants them to follow him?

# TUAREG

## BLUE-VEILED GUARDIANS OF THE SAHARA

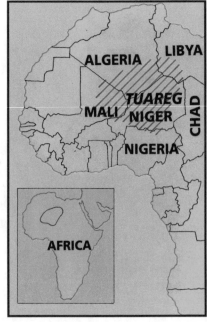

### Famine of no hope

'How different our lives are now.' Amud stopped hoeing between the millet plants and pulled his blue veil across his mouth as he spoke. 'Once we had slaves to look after our gardens, while we travelled across the desert with our camels, herds and families. Several years without rain destroyed our pasture lands. The drought brought famine and many of our people and animals starved to death. It was the worst famine we had ever known, and we called it "the famine of no hope". Now we are poor. We no longer have slaves to grow our millet and vegetables. At least I still have my own tent.'

Amud's round leather tent has been his home for many years. 'We used to carry our tents and belongings from place to place on the backs of our camels. We were proud to be called the Lords of the desert. In our own language we call ourselves *Ismahagen*, which means "noble and free", but *Tuareg*, our Arabic name, means "those abandoned by God". That is how we feel now.'

### Proud nomads

The Tuareg are nomads, descendants of the Berbers of North Africa. Many centuries ago they were driven south into the Sahara Desert and to the Sahel by Arab invaders. The Tuareg were a strong and powerful people, afraid of no one. Soon they forced the black Africans in the lands where they settled

to become their slaves.

This proud race of people became very wealthy. They spent their days raiding, trading and herding. With their herds of camels, cattle, sheep and goats, they moved through the desert from one grazing land to another. For a fee, they guided and protected traders crossing the Sahara between west and north Africa. These blue-veiled guardians of the desert were greatly feared, but they feared no one.

All this changed when France took control of large areas of West Africa in the 19th century.

To start with, they banned raiding, which had always been a part of Tuareg life. They enforced the boundaries between countries, so the Tuareg were no longer able to move freely from place to place. The power of the proud Tuareg was beginning to weaken.

## DO YOU KNOW?

The blue turban and veil of the Tuareg man is about 3 metres long. He covers his mouth with his veil when he meets anyone he respects, and when he eats he uses his left hand to lift the veil from his mouth.

## You Can Pray for the Tuareg

### Dear Lord Jesus

1 Please show Christian workers practical ways to love and care for the Tuareg, so that they may know that you have not abandoned them.

2 Send more evangelists, pastors and missionaries who can teach the new Christians your ways.

3 Help the Christians to be strong and trust you, because they are so few.

4 Give Christians the courage to tell others about the ways in which you have helped them.

5 Encourage the Christians to read the Scripture portions that have been translated into Tamashek.

6 Many Tuareg people have lost all their camels and herds and have become very poor. Please give wisdom to the aid agencies to know the best ways to help them.

7 Please send rain each year, so that the Tuareg and other tribes who live in the Sahara and Sahel will have enough food to eat.

## No longer powerful

The last fifty years have been very hard for the Tuareg. When the French gave independence to Mali, the black Africans in the south of the country came to power. The Tuareg fought the government in a civil war. They were defeated, and many of them were killed. The harsh climate defeated them, too. There is never much rain in the Sahel, but for six years there was no rain at all. Most of the animals and many people died. Large numbers of Tuareg were forced to abandon their nomadic life and go to refugee camps. There they felt they were being treated unfairly. The power of the proud Tuareg had been broken.

Do you think God has abandoned the Tuareg? They are Muslims, but, because they moved from place to place, they rarely built mosques and most of them do not keep Ramadan, the Muslim holy fast. Yet when they moved to a new place, they would invite a Muslim holy man to pray for them. Until recently few of them had heard about the Lord Jesus.

Biga listened carefully to the gospel recording in Tamashek, the language of the Tuareg. He had never heard such a wonderful story before. Did God really love men and women so much that he sent Jesus, his only Son, to die for them? Could he really change men's lives? Would he really help them every day? One day Biga asked Jesus into his life. Some people laughed at him for following the white man's religion. Soon they realized, however, that Biga was a different person because God had changed him. There are still only a few Tuareg Christians, but they are determined to show others that God loves them and will never leave them.

When Christian organizations started to send food and aid to the Tuareg, the Christians made sure that the neediest people got their share. 'How can we become followers of Jesus?' some asked. 'Although life is very hard, we see that God has not abandoned us!'

# WODAABE

## BEAUTIFUL NOMADS OF THE SAHEL

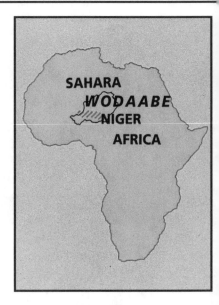

SAHARA
WODAABE
NIGER
AFRICA

of their diet. Often the animals have so little food that they become weak and do not give much milk. Then the people become very hungry and ill. While the men look after the cattle, the women are kept busy collecting firewood, milking the cows, pounding millet and cooking porridge.

### Wodaabe taboos

The Wodaabe have many customs or rules that would seem strange to us. These are called *taboos*, or things they must not do. The name Wodaabe actually means 'the people of the *taboo*'.

Are you the oldest child in your family? How would you feel if your mother was never allowed to talk to you, or call you by name? It would not matter where you came in the family, you would not have a proper name until you were twelve years old.

In countries like Britain, we are taught to look a person in the eye when we talk to him, but the Wodaabes are forbidden to do this. A man may not even hold hands with his wife, or call her by name when other people are around. These are just a few of the many taboos that control their lives.

One Sunday morning three young Wodaabe men walked into a church in Niger. They did not sit down on the seats nearest the door, as strangers usually do, but walked right to the front of the church. Everyone was quiet. Who were these three young men who looked so poor? What was going to happen? 'Will you show us how to follow the Christian way?' they asked the congregation. 'We want you to teach us and our children about Jesus!'

The Wodaabe live in the Sahel region of Niger, on the edge of the Sahara Desert. Sahel means 'the shore of the desert'. They

are nomads, and wander from place to place through this hot, dry, desert area, driving their cattle, sheep and goats. During the long, dry season they will often walk for five hours a day, searching for water and pasture. All their belongings go with them on the backs of their camels and donkeys. 'We are like birds in a bush,' a village elder explained. 'We never settle down, and we leave no trace of where we've been. If strangers come too close, we fly to another tree.'

Their food is simple. They eat porridge made from millet, but milk is the most important part

# Celebration!

The Wodaabe think they are the most beautiful people on earth! We might not agree with them, but to Wodaabe men their beauty is very important. Every year they hold special celebrations to show off their good looks. Each one wants to be thought the most handsome!

On the day of the festival the men prepare themselves very carefully. First of all they rub yellow powder on their faces, to make their skin look lighter. Then they outline their lips and eyes with a black substance called *kohl*. They shave the hair from the front of their heads, so that they appear to have very high foreheads, for this is a sign of great beauty. As a finishing touch, they paint a line from forehead to chin, to make their noses look longer. To be absolutely sure that they have done everything they can to make themselves as beautiful as possible, they wear magic powders in little

bags hung round their necks. Finally, they put on their lovely hand-embroidered robes, charms, and copper and brass jewellery, hung with beads and cowrie shells.

When all is ready, they dance together before their admiring audience. They roll their eyes and flash their teeth. Perhaps we would feel they were pulling faces, but they believe it makes them more beautiful and charming!

For many years missionaries have tried to tell the Wodaabe about the Lord Jesus, who can make them into new people. A few, like the young men who came into the church, have discovered that Jesus can indeed change them, and they want their families to know about him, too. The Wodaabe want to be beautiful on the outside. One day may they learn that only Jesus can make them beautiful on the inside.

## DO YOU KNOW?

The Wodaabe and their cattle, goats, sheep and camels, often walk as much as 1,000 miles a year in their search for water and pasture in the Sahel.

## You Can Pray for the Wodaabe

### Dear Lord Jesus

1 Please help missionaries to teach the few Wodaabe Christians, so that they will know how to follow you.

2 Send more missionaries to help the Wodaabe, and help them as they learn the Fulfulde language.

3 Help missionaries who are recording gospel cassettes to make them so interesting that many Wodaabe people will want to listen to them.

4 As they listen to your Word on cassettes, help the believers to understand and obey what they hear.

5 Help the Wodaabe people to understand that you want to give them clean hearts and make them new people.

6 Bring whole families to trust in you, so that they can help one another.

7 May the beauty of Jesus shine from the believers, so that others will also want to follow him.

# YANOMAMO

## THE CHILDREN OF THE MOON

The Yanomamo people live deep in the tropical rain forests of Amazonia. About 15,000 of them live in southern Venezuela, and another 3,000 over the border in Brazil.

### The Fierce People

They have a legend that, many, many years ago, one of the first creatures on earth shot the moon with his arrow. The moon's blood fell to earth, and where the blood fell it turned into the first people – the Yanomamo. Since they were born as a result of the shooting of the moon, they believe they were born to be fierce. So they call themselves the Fierce People, as well as the Children of the Moon.

The Yanomamo live up to their name as the Fierce People. One village fights another village, and their quarrels never seem to come to an end. When they get ready to raid a village, the Yanomamo men smear themselves with charcoal and poison the tips of their arrows with curare.

### Afraid!

Although they are fierce, they are often afraid. They are afraid of their enemies. They are afraid of bad spirits, which, they think, have been sent by their enemies to hurt them or make them ill. They are afraid of spirits in the jungle, in the water, in the dark of night. They are afraid of the jaguar living in the forest. They are even afraid to point at the moon – in case their fingers rot and fall off!

When anyone is sick, or feels that bad spirits have been sent to attack them, the witchdoctor calls on other spirits for help.

He'll call on spirits for help, too, when one village wants to attack another with sickness.

### Not worth much!

Almost as soon as Little Girl could walk, she had to go out with her mother to collect firewood in a small basket on her back. She was often tired and her legs ached. No one took much notice. After all, some girl babies are killed as soon as they're born. Little girls are not worth much!

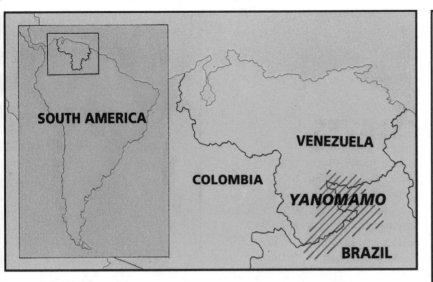

SOUTH AMERICA

VENEZUELA

COLOMBIA

YANOMAMO

BRAZIL

## DO YOU KNOW?

Thousands of Yanomamo have died in recent years because their rivers have been poisoned by mercury, which is used by illegal gold miners. Others have died from diseases the 'white men' have taken into the jungle.

One day, when she was only four, a man from another village asked her father if he could have her. He wanted her to be his wife. In exchange, he gave her father a dog. Now Little Girl has to look after the men in her new family, gather the firewood, cook for them and look after the gardens. She has to work hard and is often hungry. Little girls are not worth much!

## Village life

Every two or three years each Yanomamo village builds a new house, called a *shabano*. It is built in a circle round a large open courtyard. Each family collects trees, vines and thatch from the jungle to build the part of the roof under which his family will live. Each family's section opens out to the central courtyard. There are no dividing walls between the sections. The only wall is the outside one, separating the village from the jungle. Little entrances are left in this wall, so that people can get out of the village. There's no privacy in a Yanomamo village!

Outside the village they cut down the jungle to make fields for their manioc, plantains, gourds and sweet potatoes. While the women look after the fields, the men hunt wild pigs, tapir, armadillo and monkeys in the jungle for food.

## Leave them alone!

In Venezuela, the homeland of the Yanomamo has been made into a special reserve for them. 'The Yanomamo must be left as they are,' some people declare. 'They must be allowed to live as they have always lived. We do not want evangelical Christians, or anyone else, to come and make them change their ways. They have their own beliefs.'

In 1950 workers from the New Tribes Mission began Christian work among the Yanomamo. They helped the villagers when they were sick. They prayed, and learned all they could about them. They listened, and wrote down the Yanomamo language. It was a difficult job, and only a few seemed interested in hearing about God, the Great Spirit, who loves them.

But God is changing lives. Now there are about 300 Yanomamo Christians in Venezuela, and more in Brazil. Some, like Maloco, want to tell others about Jesus. He was only eight years old when he came to know Jesus as his friend. 'Don't laugh at me because I'm small,' he said. 'I want to share God's Word. I'm going to tell everybody they ought to believe in Jesus.'

## You Can Pray for the Yanomamo

### Dear Lord Jesus

1 Show the Yanomamo believers that you can stop them being afraid, and can free them from the power of the evil spirits.

2 Help them to live in peace, instead of fighting and killing one another.

3 Help the women and girls to know that they are valuable to you.

4 May your Holy Spirit help the Christians to live like Jesus did, and keep them from sliding back into their old ways.

5 Give the Yanomamo Christians great happiness in knowing you. May they be as ready to tell others about you as they used to be to fight them.

6 Thank you for the New Testament in Yanomamo. Help the Christians to be eager to learn to read, so that they can read your Word for themselves, and can also write down and preserve their culture.

7 May Yanomamo Christians learn how to be pastors and evangelists who can teach others to follow only you.

# YAO

## WHO TRADED IN SLAVES

### Slave trade

David Livingstone, the famous missionary-explorer, was resting after his journey when he heard a commotion. A long line of captives, men, women and children, was being driven into the village. Their captors were Yao, armed with muskets and blowing long tin horns. When they saw Dr. Livingstone, the armed men fled into the forest.

'Who are you? Where do you come from?' the doctor asked the captives.

'We are Manganja, the people of the Lake,' they told him. 'The Yao captured us, planning to sell us as slaves. They

killed many of our people and burned our houses to the ground.'

The captives were cut free, and the missionaries took care of them. Dr. Livingstone hated the slave trade, but he did not realize then that, by helping the Manganja (pronounce it *Mangan-ja*), he had made enemies of the Yao.

The Yao live at the southern end of huge Lake Malawi, in the central African country we now call Malawi. They used to trade with Arab and Portuguese merchants on the coast of East Africa, and bartered slaves, ivory and tobacco for guns and gunpowder, cloth and beads.

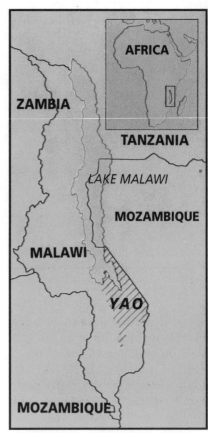

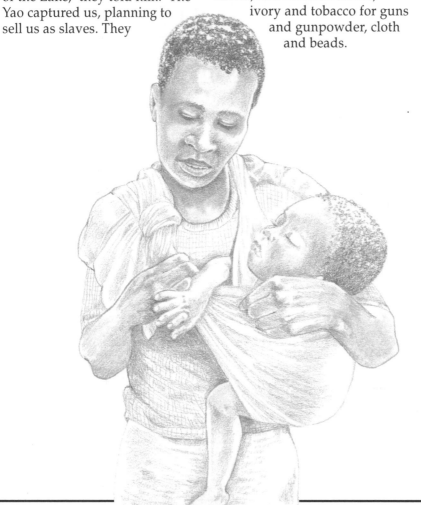

They soon realized that missionaries, as well as the British Government, were determined to stop the trade in slaves. 'We will not let the British interfere with the way we live,' they declared. 'The missionaries say they want to help us. They even say they will build schools for us and teach our children, but they will make us become Christians and their words will steal our hearts. We would have to change our ways, because we would not be able to capture and sell slaves any more.'

So the Yao people decided they would become Muslims, like the Arab traders on the coast, because they knew that then they would be able to go on trading in slaves. Even when the slave trade was abolished, not many Yao went to school, because the schools were run by Christian missionaries.

# Christian radio

The Yao love their own culture and music, and FEBA Radio have recorded some of their songs. Several Yao Christians have written special songs with Christian words, using the Yao rhythms, drums and other musical instruments. In this way, the Yao have started to learn some of the things about God which they did not know before.

William works as a caretaker in a hospital in Malawi. He used to be a Muslim, but enjoyed listening to the Christian radio programmes. 'What I am hearing is good, but there are things I don't understand,' he thought. One day, to the surprise of the programme's producer, William walked into the FEBA Radio office in Blantyre and started asking questions. 'What is the difference between a Muslim and a Christian?' he asked. 'Can you explain what you mean when you talk about God the Father, God the Son and God the Holy Spirit? That sounds like three Gods to me, but you say they are only one.'

'Dear Lord, please help me to explain the Trinity to William,' the producer prayed. Then he said to William, 'Do you think I am only a radio producer? I am more than that. I look after two churches and the Christians call me their pastor. And that is not all. I have seven children and they call me father.' He smiled. 'I am only one person, but different people think of me in different ways. God is like that. Do you understand now?'

William's face shone. 'Yes, now I do,' he said. 'I shall be able to explain all this to my friends.' He had many more questions to ask before he left for the long bus journey to his home. As William left, the programme producer prayed again. 'Dear Lord, please let all that William has learned reach his heart, and use our programmes to reach many more Yao people with the gospel.'

## DO YOU KNOW?

To show respect when shaking hands with another person, a Yao man grips his right elbow with his left hand. Women and children kneel to greet men and older people.

## You Can Pray for the Yao

### Dear Lord Jesus

1 May many Yao people forget their past and open their hearts to your love and care.

2 Use Yao pastors and evangelists to preach and teach your Word clearly.

3 Help Yao Christians to be faithful in their witness to their Muslim friends, and to the refugees from Mozambique.

4 Be with those who produce the radio programmes, and help them to make them so interesting that many people will want to listen to them.

5 Please use the radio programmes to explain the Christian faith to the people who listen to them.

6 When they do not understand all they hear on the programmes, may they ask questions, just as William did.

7 Help those who are translating the Bible into the Yao language, so that people will find it easy to understand.

# CHRISTIANITY

There are more than 1,734,000,000 people in the world today who call themselves Christians. The first time the followers of Jesus Christ were called Christians was in the city of Antioch (Acts 11:26). It was probably a nickname, but ever since then his followers have been called Christians.

## Jesus, sent from God

Jesus was born in Bethlehem in Judea during the reign of the Roman Emperor, Caesar Augustus. God told Mary his mother, and his foster father Joseph, that this baby was special. He was God's very own Son, the promised Messiah.

When Jesus was 30 years old the prophet, John the Baptist, baptized him in the River Jordan. John was baptizing people who had repented of their sins, but Jesus was sinless. After he was baptized, the Holy Spirit came on Jesus and God spoke to him from heaven.

Jesus chose twelve men to be his disciples. They travelled with him round the countryside. Jesus taught the people they met about God's love and the way he wanted them to live. He told them to turn their backs on their own way of doing things and to start living God's way because he was their true King. Jesus healed many sick people as well.

After a while Peter, one of the disciples, realized that Jesus was the Messiah whom God had promised and the Jews had been expecting for many long years.

The Jewish leaders did not like Jesus' teaching. They arrested him, accused him of blasphemy and took him to the Roman leaders. He was condemned to die, and was crucified on a cross like a thief or a murderer. But that was not the end. Three days later Jesus rose from the dead. Over the next forty days many people saw him, first some of the women who followed him, then the disciples and later on, whole crowds of people. Then Jesus returned to his Father in heaven, where he is alive for evermore.

## What Christians believe

When God made man and woman, he made them perfect. He wanted them to be his friends and he promised to care for them. But people chose to do what they wanted instead of the good things God wanted. This is sin, and so sin came into God's perfect world.

Every one of us sins. Sin doesn't only mean telling lies, or stealing or murdering someone. We all want to go our own way, and live our lives the way we want, and we often think God doesn't matter. That is sin.

God is pure and holy, but our sin is like a huge heap of rubbish that stops us from reaching him. But God loves us and wants us to be his friends. So he sent his Son, Jesus, who had never done any wrong, to earth. Then God took all our sins and dumped them on Jesus.

This is what was really happening when Jesus died on the cross. He destroyed that huge heap of sin. Now the path to God is open and we can know his love and care. Christians know Jesus as their very special friend who will always look after them and help them.

All round the world Christians are full of joy because Jesus rose from the dead and is alive today. Now he is in heaven with God where he is praying for us, but one day he will come back to earth. When Jesus went back to heaven he sent his Holy Spirit to help people to know him. When we become Christians the Holy Spirit lives in us and helps us to live the way God wants and to tell others about him. He is always with us and will help us even when life is hard. When we die, we will go to live with God in heaven.

## Churches

There are many kinds of Christian churches. Some, such as the Orthodox, Roman Catholic, Protestant and Evangelical churches, are mentioned in this book. The ways in which they worship God are different. Some Christians meet in huge, ornate cathedrals, while others worship him in very simple buildings.

But the real church is not just buildings. It is made up of true Christians wherever they live in the world. These are men, women and children who have asked Jesus Christ to be their Saviour and Lord, and who always try to please him.

# JUDAISM

Judaism is the religion of the Jewish people. Their beliefs are based on the Old Testament. They call the first five books of the Old Testament the Torah (or teachings). Each year the whole of the Torah is read in synagogues, the Jewish places of worship.

Over many years the teachings of the Rabbis (religious teachers) were collected together. This collection is called the Talmud, and has become as important to many Jewish people as the scriptures.

The Jews believe that God is the creator of heaven and earth, and that everything, and everyone, exists by his command. They believe that man is created in the image of God, and that they are God's chosen people. He gave them a set of moral rules to show them how they should live, but he also gave them free will so they could make their own choices. Men and women are responsible for the choices they make.

## The beginning

God chose one man, Abraham, and his family to be his people. God told Abraham to leave his own country and go to the land he would show him (Genesis 12:1-3). God promised Abraham that he would bless him and make him a great nation. He also promised Abraham that all the peoples of the world would be blessed through him.

## A chosen nation

Hundreds of years passed, and Abraham's descendants became slaves in Egypt. God chose Moses to lead them out of Egypt to the promised land. (You can read the story for yourself in Exodus chapters 1-19.) God told Moses that if the people of Israel obeyed him in everything, they would be his special people. God wanted them to be different from all the other nations who worshipped many gods. He wanted them to worship him alone.

God chose them to be holy, like himself. He gave them a set of rules, called the Ten Commandments, to keep, and promised to bless and help them if they were obedient to him. If they did not keep God's rules, they would be punished.

Throughout their history, the Jewish people have seen everything that has happened to them as the work of God, leading his people onwards. God has shown them his love and care, guided and punished them. They have been sent into exile, and scattered to the far corners of the earth. Wherever they have lived and whatever they have suffered, they have kept their identity as Jews.

In their suffering they have looked for God's promised Deliverer or Messiah, to lead them back to their own land and to bring peace and justice on earth. Many are still waiting for him to come.

## Worship

The first prayer a Jewish child learns, and says every morning, comes from Deuteronomy 6. In synagogues this same prayer is recited morning and evening. It is this: 'Hear, O Israel: the Lord our God is one Lord; and you shall love the Lord your God with all your heart, and with all your soul, and with all your might.'

Throughout the year there are many Jewish festivals which celebrate special events in the Old Testament calendar, such as the feast of the Passover, the Feast of Tabernacles and the Day of Atonement. Every week the Sabbath is kept.

The Sabbath begins at dusk on Friday and ends at dusk on Saturday. It is a holy day, a day of rest, when Jews remember that God rested from his work of creation on the seventh day. Often the men and boys go to the synagogue on Friday evening before the Sabbath meal, and again on Saturday morning.

At the evening meal on Friday, the mother lights candles and blesses God. The father takes a cup of wine and says a blessing for his family. Everyone receives a piece of bread and eats it with salt. This reminds them that God supplied his people with manna during their wanderings in the wilderness. After all this has been done, the meal begins.

While some Jewish people still wait for the Messiah to come, others do not believe in a Messiah at all. Christians, whose beliefs and knowledge of God are firmly based on the Old Testament, are sure that Jesus is the Messiah promised by God.

# WORD LIST

**agent:** a person who does something on your behalf instead of your having to do it yourself.

**agnostic:** a person who says we do not know and cannot know that God exists.

**ancestor cult:** the worship of people's ancestors (dead relatives) because the people believe that these ancestors are alive and powerful.

**armadillo:** an animal whose body is covered in bony plates like armour. It burrows in the ground and can roll itself into a ball.

**atheist:** someone who thinks that there is no God.

**autonomous:** self-governing.

**blasphemy:** saying evil or wrong things about God or holy things.

**Bolshevik:** (Russian) people who wanted the government of the country to be by the workers for the workers.

**cacao:** the tree or the seed from which cocoa and chocolate are made.

**calypso:** a West Indian song with an African rhythm. The words are often made up by the singer as he sings.

**carousel:** a conveyor belt that goes round in a circle. (You collect your luggage from one of these at an airport.)

**caste:** a group into which a Hindu person is born. The most important is the priestly caste. The next caste are rulers and soldiers, then traders and shopkeepers. People in the lowest caste sweep, wash clothes and are generally servants of the higher castes.

**colonize:** to set up a colony.

**colony:** a group of people who have settled in a new country and may still be ruled by the country from which they have come.

**conquistadors:** Spaniards who conquered and colonized parts of South America.

**coup d'état:** a sudden or violent take-over of a government by a small group of people.

**creole:** people and languages formed from a mixture of races and languages.

**cult:** a religious group which has its own objects of worship and its own ceremonies.

**culture:** the way of life of a country or people. This includes their language and religion.

**curare:** a poison found in certain plants in South America.

**delta:** low-lying land through which a river, with many branches and mouths, flows out to the sea.

**depose:** to remove from an official job.

**dung:** animal manure.

**emigrate:** leave one's own country and go to settle in another.

**evangelical:** a Christian who believes that our only hope is to trust in Jesus who saves us from our sins. He or she believes that the whole Bible is the Word of God.

**fetish:** a 'thing' which is worshipped.

**fiord:** a narrow inlet of sea between high cliffs.

**gourd:** the large fruit of a rambling plant. The fruit is often dried and the outside used as a bottle or container.

**griddle:** a round iron plate which is placed over heat and used for baking.

**guerrilla:** a member of a rebel army. He may work on his own or in a small group.

**imam:** leader of prayer in a mosque.

**immigrant:** a person who has left his or her own country and come to live permanently in another country.

**jihad:** the Muslim name for a holy war fought against those considered enemies of Allah.

**jute:** fibre from the jute plant which is used to make rope, string and sacking.

**kayak:** an Eskimo one-man canoe.

**Koran:** the sacred book of Islam. (Sometimes it is spelled Qur'an.)

**machete:** a broad, heavy knife used for cutting down plants.

**manioc:** a plant grown in many tropical countries. The thick roots are used for food.

**marabout:** a Muslim leader or holy man who claims he can work miracles, heal sick people, tell fortunes, or bring curses on other people's enemies.

**martyr:** a person who dies for what he believes.

**meditate:** to keep thinking deeply about something (e.g. God).

**millet:** a very tall cereal plant with small seeds which provide good nourishment. (If you have a budgerigar you may have bought millet to feed it!)

**montagnard:** a tribal person living in the mountain region of Vietnam.

**mujahidin:** Muslim soldiers who are fighting what they believe is a 'holy war' or jihad.

**omen:** something which happens and is taken as a sign that something else will happen. Some omens mean something good will happen, but others mean that what happens will be bad or harmful.

**Orthodox Christianity:** an old form of Christianity which is still practised today, especially in countries such as Russia, Greece and Bulgaria.

**pitch:** a thick black liquid made from tar.

**plantain:** a tropical fruit which looks a bit like a banana.

**protestant:** members or followers of Christian churches which broke away from the Roman Catholic churches in the 16th century.

**raze:** completely destroy.

**republic:** a country or state which does not have a king or queen, but is ruled by a president who is elected by the people of that country.

**reserve:** an area of land kept for a special purpose. This may be as a nature reserve for birds and animals, or as the homeland for a group of tribal people.

**revolution:** the overthrow of the government by the people of that country.

**sadhu:** an Indian holy man. Some wear a simple, saffron coloured garment, but others wear only a loin cloth. Some have long hair and beards, but others shave their heads.

**Sahel:** the region at the southern edge of the Sahara Desert in Africa.

**sect:** a group of people who have turned their backs on some of the main beliefs of a religion and have formed their own beliefs.

**secular:** not religious.

**sickle:** a large knife with a semi-circular blade which is used for cutting grass or reaping plants such as wheat or rice.

**sika:** an ornamental hanger for holding bowls or dishes.

**stupa:** a Buddhist monument which may contain bones, hair or clothing of a person they want to remember. Buddhist pilgrims often visit these stupas and put small gifts and flowers in front of them.

**taboo:** something that you must not talk about, touch, have or do because of your religion.

**tapir:** a pig-like animal related to the rhinoceros.

# WHAT NEXT?

### God's plan

God loves you and has a special purpose for your life. He already knows the good things he has planned for you and what he wants you to do. So why don't you ask him to show you? He can tell you what he wants you to do through something you read in his Word, the Bible, because of something that happens or that someone says.

Perhaps you are thinking, 'But I'm not sure if I really know Jesus.' But Jesus knows all about you and longs for you to ask him to be your friend! Jesus loves you and died for you because that was the only way to take away all the wrong things that get between us and God. Tell him that you want to get rid of them all. Then tell him you want to live his way and do what he wants you to do. You can be sure that he will help you!

### Get to know Jesus

Spend time getting to know Jesus. Talk with him and listen to what he says and learn to obey him. Read the Bible and learn his Word by heart. His Holy Spirit will help you to pray and tell others about him.

### Read

• You can find out more about the countries and people groups in this book by writing to the agencies on page 123.
• Your local library may have books about some of the countries you have read about.
• Some missionary biographies have been written specially for children. Many are very exciting, and will help you to understand what it's like to work for Jesus. Read a missionary comic. Some agencies such as Mission Aviation Fellowship and Tear Fund produce comics about their work. CHIME publishes a monthly missionary comic. Reading is fun!

### Look!

• Watch the news on TV.
• Watch travel programmes.
• Look through magazines for pictures of the countries and people you have been learning about.

### Make friends

• If missionaries come to your church, make friends with them. Listen to what they say. Ask them questions and find out how you and your church or Sunday school can help them. Write to them and if they have children write to them as well. They will like that.
• Make friends with someone in your church who comes from another country, because he or she may feel very lonely.
• Make friends with someone in your class at school who isn't a Christian. Perhaps you will be able to show them the way to know Jesus.

### Pray

Remember that God wants us to pray and to share with him in his work. Sometimes it is hard for us to keep on praying, but here are a few ideas to help you.
• Choose seven different topics, countries, people groups or individuals. Write them on separate pages in a notebook and pray for one each day of the week.
• When you know a prayer has been answered, write that in your notebook, too.
• Get a world map. Mark on it the places you pray for. Add some pictures of the people you pray for as well.
• It helps to pray with someone else: a friend, your family or in Sunday School. You may even find a Daniel Prayer Group (King's Kids) near you.

### Go!

• Learn more about mission at a summer camp such as Warrior (10s-13s) and Teen Camps run by WEC International.
• Perhaps you or your whole family could visit a country that interests you and where your missionary friends work.
• When you're on holiday, pray for the people you meet who don't know Jesus.
• Some organizations, such as King's Kids (YWAM), have special outreaches using teenagers.
• Does Jesus want you to become one of his special messengers to tell others about him? Don't give up . . . . He will show you how and where and when.

### For more ideas write to:

**Children's Resources Worker (CRW)**
WEC International
Bulstrode
Oxford Road
Gerrards Cross
Bucks, SL9 8SZ

**CHIME (Children in Mission and Evangelism)**
14 Queens Road
Teddington
Middlesex, TW11 0LR

**King's Kids**
Stanely House
14 Stanely Crescent
Paisley
Scotland
PA2 9LF

# SOME FACTS
## ABOUT THE PEOPLES IN THIS BOOK

| People | Estimated numbers | Main religions | Main countries in which they live |
|---|---|---|---|
| Aceh* | 2,900,000 | Islam | Indonesia (Sumatra) |
| Balinese* | 3,800,000 | Hinduism | Indonesia (Bali) |
| Beja* | 1,585,000 | Islam | Sudan |
| Bijago* | 24,500 | Animism | Guinea-Bissau |
| Buryat* | 468,000 | Buddhism | Russia, Mongolia |
| Chakma | 663,600 | Buddhism | Bangladesh, India |
| Dai* | 1,025,000 | Buddhism | China |
| Dayak* | 2,900,000 | Animism, Christianity | Indonesia (Kalimantan) |
| Druze | 500,000 | Druze | Syria, Lebanon, Israel |
| Garifuna* | 82,000 | Animism, Christianity | Belize, Honduras, Guatemala |
| Gond* | 8,349,000 | Animism, Hinduism | India |
| Hazara* | 1,870,000 | Islam | Afghanistan, Pakistan |
| Hui* | 8,603,000 | Islam | China |
| Kyrgyz* | 2,370,000 | Islam | Kyrgyzstan |
| Mandinka* | 896,000 | Islam | Gambia, Senegal, Guinea-Bissau |
| Newar* | 775,000 | Buddhism, Hinduism | Nepal |
| North Africans in France | 3,700,000 | Islam | France |
| Pygmies | 200,000 | Animism | Zaire, Central African Republic |
| Qashqa'i* | 860,000 | Islam | Iran |
| Refugees | 44,000,000 | | Worldwide |
| Rohingya* | 750,000 | Islam | Myanmar, Bangladesh |
| Sundanese* | 31,000,000 | Islam | Indonesia (Java) |
| Tuareg* | 1,500,000 | Islam | Mali, Niger, Libya |
| Wodaabe | 45,000 | Animism | Niger |
| Yanomamo | 16,000 | Animism | Venezuela, Brazil |
| Yao* | 1,716,000 | Islam | Malawi, Mozambique, Tanzania |

The figures given above are only estimates.
The information for people groups marked * has been taken from *Operation World*
(5th edition, 1993) by Patrick Johnstone.

# MORE FACTS

## ABOUT THE COUNTRIES IN THIS BOOK
### Including the main countries where the peoples in this book live

| Country | Capital | Main religious groups | Number of people | Area in square km |
|---|---|---|---|---|
| Afghanistan | Kabul | Muslim | 17,800,000 | 652,000 |
| Bangladesh | Dhaka | Muslim, Hindu | 116,600,000 | 144,000 |
| Belize | Belmopan | Christian | 200,000 | 23,000 |
| Bulgaria | Sofia | Orthodox Christian, Muslim | 8,400,000 | 111,000 |
| China | Beijing | Atheist, Christian, Muslim, Chinese Religions | 1,192,000,000 | 9,573,000 |
| Colombia | Santa Fe de Bogotá | Christian | 35,600,000 | 1,139,000 |
| Cuba | Havana | Atheist, Roman Catholic, Spiritism | 11,100,000 | 115,000 |
| Egypt | Cairo | Muslim, Coptic Christian | 58,900,000 | 1,001,000 |
| Equatorial Guinea | Malabo | Roman Catholic | 400,000 | 28,000 |
| France | Paris | Secular, Roman Catholic | 58,000,000 | 551,000 |
| Gambia | Banjul | Muslim | 1,100,000 | 11,300 |
| Greenland (OW, 1993) | Nuuk | Christian | 58,000 | 2,176,000 |
| Guinea-Bissau | Bissau | Muslim, Animist | 1,100,000 | 36,000 |
| Honduras | Tegucigalpa | Roman Catholic | 5,300,000 | 112,000 |
| Iceland | Reykjavik | Christian | 300,000 | 103,000 |
| India | New Delhi | Secular, Hindu, Muslim | 911,600,000 | 3,204,000 |
| Indonesia | Jakarta | Muslim, Christian | 199,700,000 | 1,920,000 |
| Iran | Tehran | Muslim | 61,200,000 | 1,648,000 |
| Iraq | Baghdad | Muslim | 19,900,000 | 435,000 |
| Israel | Jerusalem | Jewish, Muslim | *5,400,000 | *20,700 |
| Korea (North) | Pyongyang | Atheist | 23,100,000 | 123,000 |
| Kyrgyzstan | Bishkek | Muslim, Secular | 4,500,000 | 199,000 |

| Country | Capital | Main religious groups | Number of people | Area in square km |
|---|---|---|---|---|
| Lebanon | Beirut | Muslim, Orthodox Christian | 3,600,000 | 10,400 |
| Madagascar | Antananarivo | Christian, Traditional Religions | 13,700,000 | 587,000 |
| Malawi | Lilongwe | Christian, Muslim | 9,500,000 | 118,000 |
| Maldives | Malé | Muslim | 200,000 | 298 |
| Mali | Bamako | Muslim | 9,100,000 | 1,240,000 |
| Myanmar (Burma) | Yangon | Buddhist | 45,400,000 | 677,000 |
| Nepal | Kathmandu | Hindu, Buddhist | 22,100,000 | 141,000 |
| New Caledonia | Nouméa | Christian, Secular | 200,000 | 18,700 |
| Niger | Niamey | Muslim | 8,800,000 | 1,267,000 |
| Republic of Guinea | Conakry | Muslim, Animist | 6,400,000 | 246,000 |
| Russia | Moscow | Secular, Orthodox Christian | 147,800,000 | 17,075,000 |
| Saudi Arabia | Riyadh | Muslim | 18,000,000 | 2,240,000 |
| Spain | Madrid | Roman Catholic, Secular | 39,200,000 | 505,000 |
| Sudan | Khartoum | Muslim, Christian | 28,200,000 | 2,504,000 |
| Syria | Damascus | Muslim | 14,000,000 | 185,000 |
| Trinidad & Tobago | Port-of-Spain | Christian, Hindu | 1,300,000 | 5,128 |
| Uruguay | Montevideo | Secular, Christian | 3,200,000 | 176,000 |
| Venezuela | Caracas | Roman Catholic | 21,300,000 | 912,000 |
| Vietnam | Hanoi | Buddhist, Secular | 73,100,000 | 330,000 |
| Zaire | Kinshasa | Christian, Animist | 42,500,000 | 2,345,000 |

* These figures do not include the West Bank, Gaza Strip or the Golan Heights.

With the exception of Greenland, the population figures are taken from the World Population Data Sheet (1994) of the Population Reference Bureau, Inc.

# IF YOU WANT TO FIND OUT MORE . . .

Here is a list of some agencies which may be able to help you. We have just used their initials and you will find their addresses on page 123. If you want to find out more about a people group, find out what country it is in first.

These are the kinds of things they might have: information for children, information for adults, activity packs for children, packs for leaders of children's groups, leaflets, pictures, books, worksheets, videos, people who can tell you more and answer your questions.

| Country/Subject | Christian Agency | Country/Subject | Christian Agency |
|---|---|---|---|
| Afghanistan | FEBA PI TF WEC* | Madagascar | AEF AIM MAF |
| Bangladesh | FEBA TF TLM YWAM | Malawi | FEBA LR |
| Belize | LR TF | Maldives | |
| Bulgaria | CLC WEC YWAM | Mali | LR TF YWAM |
| China | OMF TF WEC* YWAM | Missionary Kids | AWM WEC* |
| Colombia | OMS WBT WEC* YWAM | Myanmar (Burma) | CLC |
| Cuba | CLC TF | Nepal | INF* IS TF |
| Egypt | AP AWM FEBA MECO TF* YWAM | New Caledonia | WBT YWAM |
| Equatorial Guinea | WEC YWAM | Niger | SIM YWAM |
| France (North Africans) | AWM SIM WEC* | Refugees | AIM* IS TF* WEC* |
| Greenland | NTM YWAM | Republic of Guinea | NTM SIM TF TLM WEC* |
| Guinea-Bissau | TF WEC* YWAM | Russia | OMS TF WEC* YWAM |
| Iceland | YWAM | Saudi Arabia | AWM FEBA WEC* |
| India | IS OMS TF* WEC* YWAM | Spain | AP ECM OMS UFM WEC* |
| Indonesia | OMF* WEC* YWAM | Sudan | AIM |
| Iran | | Syria | AWM FEBA MECO |
| Iraq | AWM FEBA MECO TF YWAM | Trinidad & Tobago | CLC |
| Israel | CMJ CWI FEBA | Uruguay | CLC WEC YWAM |
| Korea (North) | | Venezuela | NTM WEC* YWAM |
| Kyrgyzstan | PI WEC* YWAM | Vietnam | WEC* |
| Lebanon | MECO WEC | Zaire | WBT WEC |

N.B. Agencies marked * may have some material for children.

# ADDRESS LIST

*Agencies marked * have some special materials and information available for children and young people. However, it may not be about the country or people group you are interested in.*

**AEF**
Africa Evangelical
Fellowship
30 Lingfield Road
Wimbledon
London
SW19 4PU

**AIM***
Africa Inland Mission
2 Vorley Road
Archway
London
N19 5HE

**AP**
Action Partners
Bawtry Hall
Bawtry
Doncaster
DN10 6JH

**AWM***
Arab World Ministries
PO Box 51
Loughborough
Leics.
LE11 0ZQ

**CLC***
Christian Literature
Crusade
Children's Dept.
201 Church Road
Upper Norwood
London
SE19 2PT

**CMJ**
Church's Ministry
Among the Jews
30c Clarence Road
St. Albans
Herts.
AL1 4JJ

**CWI**
Christian Witness to
Israel
166 Main Road
Sundridge
Sevenoaks
Kent
TN14 6EL

**ECM**
European Christian
Mission
50 Billing Road
Northampton
NN1 5DH

**FEBA***
FEBA Radio
Ivy Arch Road
Worthing
West Sussex
BN14 8BX

**INF***
International Nepal
Fellowship
69 Wentworth Road
Harborne
Birmingham
B17 9SS

**IS**
Interserve
325 Kennington Road
London
SE11 4QH

**LR**
Language Recordings
PO Box 197
High Wycombe
Bucks.
HP14 3YY

**MAF***
Mission Aviation
Fellowship
Ingles Manor
Castle Hill Avenue
Folkestone
Kent
C20 2TN

**MECO***
Middle East Christian
Outreach
22 Culverdon Park Road
Tunbridge Wells
Kent
TN4 9RA

**NTM**
New Tribes Mission
Cromford Court
Matlock Bath
Matlock
Derbyshire
DE4 3PY

**OM**
Operation Mobilisation
The Quinta
Weston Rhyn
Oswestry
Shropshire
SY10 7LT

**OMF***
OMF International (UK)
Belmont
The Vine
Sevenoaks
Kent
TN13 3TZ

**OMS**
OMS International
1 Sandileigh Avenue
Didsbury
Manchester
M20 3LN

**PI***
People International
Worldwide
PO Box 151
Tonbridge
Kent
TN11 9XL

**SIM**
SIM-UK
Ullswater Crescent
Coulsdon
Surrey
CR5 2HR

**TF***
Tear Fund
100 Church Road
Teddington
Middlesex
TW11 8QE

**TLM***
The Leprosy Mission
Goldhay Way
Orton Goldhay
Peterborough
PE2 5GZ

**UFM***
UFM Worldwide
47A Fleet Street
Swindon
SN1 1RE

**WBT**
Wycliffe Bible Translators
Wycliffe Centre
Horsleys Green
High Wycombe
Bucks
HP14 3XL

**WEC***
WEC International
Children's Resources
Bulstrode
Oxford Road
Gerrards Cross
Bucks.
SL9 8SZ

**YWAM**
Youth With a Mission
National Office
Highfield Oval
Harpenden
Herts.
AL5 4BX

If you have any difficulty
in obtaining information,
please contact the
Children's Resources
Worker at WEC
International.

# PRAY FOR THE WORLD

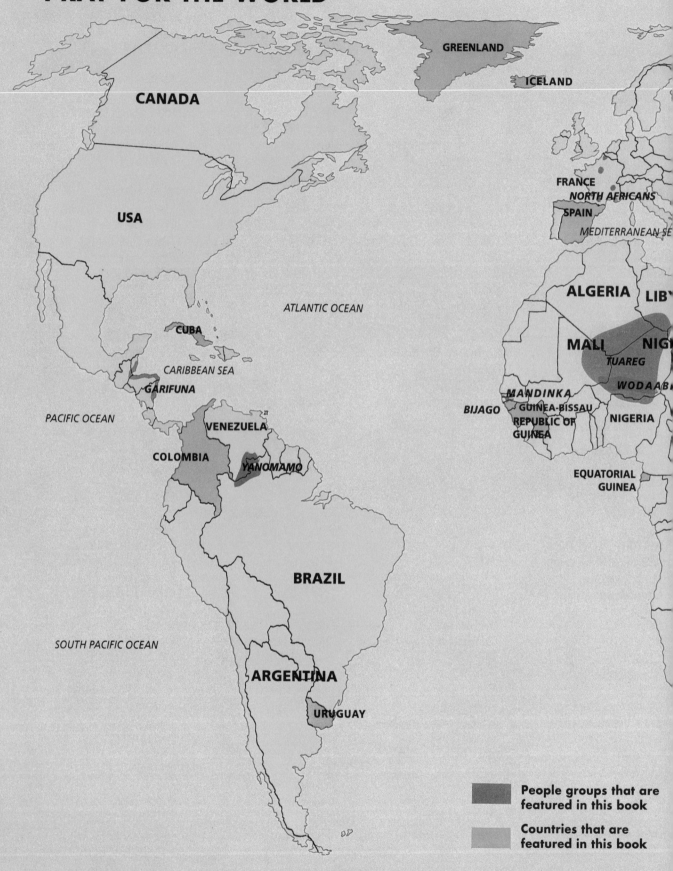

GREENLAND

ICELAND

CANADA

FRANCE
NORTH AFRICANS

SPAIN

MEDITERRANEAN SE

USA

ATLANTIC OCEAN

ALGERIA    LIB

CUBA

MALI     NIG

TUAREG

CARIBBEAN SEA

WODAAB

GARIFUNA

MANDINKA
GUINEA-BISSAU

PACIFIC OCEAN

BIJAGO    REPUBLIC OF
GUINEA

NIGERIA

VENEZUELA

COLOMBIA

YANOMAMO

EQUATORIAL
GUINEA

BRAZIL

SOUTH PACIFIC OCEAN

ARGENTINA

URUGUAY

People groups that are
featured in this book

Countries that are
featured in this book

RUSSIA

*BURYAT*

*KYRGYZ*

NORTH KOREA

*HUI*

CHINA

ARIA

SYRIA
RUZE
SRAEL

IRAQ

IRAN

*HAZARA*

AFGHANISTAN

*QASHQA'I*

PERSIAN GULF

INDIA

*NEWAR*

BANGLADESH

*CHAKMA*

*DAI*

CHINA SEA

GYPT

SAUDI ARABIA

*GOND*

*ROHINGYA*

*BEJA*

ARABIAN SEA

JDAN

INDIAN OCEAN

VIETNAM

MALDIVES

*ACEHNESE*

GMIES

*DAYAK*

IRE

*SUNDANESE*

INDONESIA

JAVA SEA

*BALINESE*

MALAWI

*YAO*

MADAGASCAR

AUSTRALIA

NEW
CALEDONIA

125

# ACKNOWLEDGEMENTS

Jill Johnstone was convinced that children have a special part to play in praying for the world. As a result she wrote *You Can Change the World* which has given thousands of young people, families, clubs and Sunday schools a glimpse of a world in need of prayer. All round the world people have used her book to help them pray.

In May 1992, when she knew she would soon be going to be with Jesus, Jill asked me to write a second volume. She even gave me a list of the 26 countries and 26 people groups which she felt should be included. Without her vision, encouragement and challenge I would never have written this book.

First of all, I am grateful to Jill for asking me, as writing the book has been an enriching experience. As a result of many hours spent in research, I have discovered a lot about other countries and people groups. Everything I have learnt has made me want to pray more.

Many people and mission agencies have graciously answered my enquiries, provided me with valuable information and pictures, and checked the material. I am grateful to each one.

My colleagues in WEC International have supported me by their interest and prayers. In particular I am grateful to John Bardsley and Rosie Scott for their advice, and to all the staff of the International Research Office for their patience as I have asked questions and searched their files.

All round the world many people have been praying for this second book. Knowing this has been a constant source of encouragement and inspiration.

Lastly, I must thank my husband Roy, who has often spent many months on his own, ministering in other parts of the world, while I have been writing this book.

*Daphne Spraggett*

Copyright © 1996 Daphne Spraggett
Design copyright © Three's Company /Angus Hudson Ltd 1996
Published by WEC International, Bulstrode, Gerrards Cross, Bucks SL9 8SZ U.K.

All rights reserved
No part of this publication may be reproduced, stored in a retrieval system, or transmitted, in any form or by any means, electronic, mechanical, photocopying, recording, or otherwise without prior permission of the publisher or a licence permitting restricted copying. In the UK such licences are issued by The Copyright Licensing Agency, 90 Tottenham Court Road, London, WIP 9HE.

British Library Cataloguing in Publication Data
Spraggett, Daphne
You Too Can Change the World
   1. Prayer - Christianity - Juvenile Literature 2. Prayers - Juvenile Literature
   I. Title
   242

   ISBN 0-900828-76-5

Created by Three's Company, 5 Dryden Street, London WC2E 9NW

Worldwide coedition organized and produced by
Angus Hudson Ltd, Concorde House, Grenville Place, Mill Hill, London NW7 3SA

Book design by Peter Wyart
Illustrations by Tony Kenyon
Special portraits for People Groups by Mary Filidis, except those on pp. 60/61, 63, 64, 70 and 94, which are by Shirley Bellwood